LORD DUNSANY

Certainly, of all the weavers of beautiful magic, there is none like Dunsany. And perhaps his magic is so powerful because he himself believed in basing his stories in the roots of reality. Of writing he said:

"It is my belief that those sudden visionary pictures which are the true essence of any art arise like a flower from a seed that has fallen into the mind, sometimes in infancy, sometimes in later childhood, sometimes in adult years, but often as imperceptibly as any seed blown on the wind finds a home for itself in the earth at the end of its wandering. Bricks without straw are more easily made than imagination without memories."

Dunsany's life was extraordinarily rich in experience —he was globetrotter, sportsman, poet, peer, lecturer, playwright and much more. However, although he set the matrix for many a following writer of adult fantasy, the richness and individuality of his writing came from a special talent that has never been equalled or duplicated.

Adult Fantasy by
LORD DUNSANY

Published by Ballantine Books

OVER THE HILLS AND FAR AWAY

Lord Dunsany

Introduction by Lin Carter

BALLANTINE BOOKS • NEW YORK

ACKNOWLEDGEMENTS

"The Journey of the King" appeared in TIME AND THE GODS (London: William Heinemann, 1906; Boston: John W. Luce & Company).

"In the Twilight," "The Lord of Cities," "The Doom of La Traviata," "The Fall of Babbulkund," "The Highwayman," "The Ghosts," and "On the Dry Land" appeared in THE SWORD OF WELLERAN (London: Geo. Allen & Sons, 1908; Boston: John W. Luce & Company).

"Blagdaross," "Where the Tides Ebb and Flow," "Poor Old Bill," "The Field," and "The Unhappy Body" appeared in A DREAMER'S TALES (London: Geo. Allen & Sons, 1910; Boston: John W. Luce & Company).

"The House of the Sphinx" appeared in THE BOOK OF WONDER (London: William Heinemann, 1912; Boston: John W. Luce & Company, 1912).

"The Little City," "The Unpasturable Fields," "The Lonely Idol," and "The Man with Gold Earrings" appeared in FIFTY-ONE TALES (London: Elkin Mathews, 1914).

"The Bad Old Woman," "A Narrow Escape," "The Loot of Loma," "The Bird of the Difficult Eye," "The Secret of the Sea," and "How Plash-Goo Came to the Land of None's Desire" appeared in TALES OF WONDER (London: Elkin Mathews, 1916; published in the U.S. under the title of THE LAST BOOK OF WONDER, Boston: John W. Luce & Company, 1916; copyright 1916 by John W. Luce & Company).

"The Queen's Enemies" appeared in PLAYS OF GODS AND MEN (London: T. Fisher Unwin, Ltd., 1917; Boston: John W. Luce & Company, 1917).

"The Compromise of the King of the Golden Isles" appeared in PLAYS OF NEAR AND FAR (New York & London: G. P. Putnam's Sons, 1922).

"The Last Dream of Bwona Kubla," "East and West," "An Archive of the Older Mysteries," "The Gift of the Gods," "How the Gods Avenged Meoul Ki-Ning," and "The Prayer of Boob Aheera" appeared in TALES OF THREE HEMISPHERES (Boston: John W. Luce & Company, 1919; copyright 1919 by John W. Luce & Company).

"The Curse of the Witch" and "Hunting the Unicorn" (orig. "What Jorkens Has to Put up With") appeared in JORKENS REMEMBERS AFRICA (New York: Longmans, Green & Company, 1934; copyright 1934 by Lord Dunsany).

"The Pale Green Image" and "The Sacred City of Krakovlitz" appeared in THE FOURTH BOOK OF JORKENS (London: Jarrolds, n.d.; Sauk City: Arkham House, 1948; copyright 1948 by Lord Dunsany).

"On Reading Lord Dunsany's Book of Wonder," a poem by H. P. Lovecraft, first appeared in *The Silver Clarion*, the issue of March, 1920. This previously overlooked and uncollected poem, discovered by bibliographer Mark Owings, was reprinted for the first time in *Kadath/One*, a new fantasy magazine edited and published by Lin Carter; copyright © 1973 by Lin Carter.

BALLANTINE BOOKS, INC.
A Division of Random House, Inc.
201 East 50th Street, New York, N.Y. 10022

Over the Hills and Far Away

is dedicated to Lord Dunsany's
American friend and hostess,
HAZEL LITTLEFIELD SMITH
with the very best wishes of
The Editor.

Contents

III. TALES OF NEAR AT HAND

IV. TALES JORKENS TOLD

About OVER THE HILLS AND FAR
AWAY, *and Lord Dunsany:*

Happy Far-Off Things

LORD DUNSANY is probably the greatest fantasy writer
who ever lived. Quite a few of the most distinguished
writers of fantasy have made a similar judgment of his
work. James Branch Cabell, for example, praised
Dunsany's craftmanship in glowing terms. H. P. Lovecraft adored Dunsany's early *Book of Wonder* tales, and
paid them the high compliment of direct imitation (as
I also have done in my little fables of Simrana the
Dreamworld). In fact, Lovecraft wrote several pieces
about Dunsany's work, which he considered superla-
tive.* I think that Clark Ashton Smith might also have
concurred with my estimate of Dunsany, and perhaps
Jack Vance and Fritz Leiber would agree as well. I
know that my friend and sometime collaborator L.
Sprague de Camp does.

Dunsany was a British peer. His full name was
Edward John Moreton Drax Plunkett. He was born in
1878 and received his education at Eton and Sandhurst,
the British military training college. He was destined
for a career in the Army, and served during the Boer

*One of them is the poem quoted in its entirety on page 14.
This tribute, incidentally, languished in an obscure journal for
half a century, till bibliographer Mark Owings discovered it
and passed it along to me. I reprinted it initially in 1973, in the
first issue of my new fantasy magazine, *Kadath,* and have included it again here as a rare curiosity.

War with the Coldstream Guards as a front-line officer. But when he was twenty-one his father died, and he succeeded to the ancient family title, becoming the eighteenth Baron Dunsany.

At the outbreak of the First World War, Lord Dunsany was not immediately sent to the front with the expeditionary forces. Because of his valuable earlier experience as a line officer under fire in South Africa, he was retained in England to assist in the enormous task of training raw recruits for "Kitchener's army." Later, he was wounded in the Dublin riots, and had to recuperate in the Londonderry barracks; he was released, however, in time to join his regiment before it sailed for France.

Just as the peer was also a poet, so the soldier was also a sportsman. Lord Dunsany was passionately fond of hunting and shooting; he rode to hounds, went on safari in Africa to hunt lions, and was an all-around outdoorsman. In addition, his long life encompassed such richness and variety of experience that I hardly know where to begin discussing it in a brief introduction. He lectured in English Literature at Athens, narrowly escaping one jump ahead of the Nazis. He was also a famous chess player and once held the championship of Ireland, Scotland, *and* Wales. And, in that connection, I should mention that he wrote what many consider one of the very best chess stories ever written —if not actually *the* best—"Jorkens' Problem."

Which brings me to the aspect of his life with which we are mostly concerned in this book, his career as a writer. Yet even here I hardly know where to begin. Dunsany wrote novels, short stories, poems, plays, essays, and autobiography, as well as translating Horace from the Greek! I know of no fewer than *seventy* books which bear his name, and for all I know there are many more. And in each of these genres his work was extraordinary. Take his numerous plays, for instance: they were performed in Dublin, London, Moscow, and New York, often simultaneously. (In New York, he once had *five* plays running at different theatres at the same time!) And when we come to his fiction, we find that he wrote a little of just about everything: novels of contemporary life, tales of heroic fantasy, murder mysteries, science fiction, and social comedy. There are tales thoughful, humorous, idyllic, serious, preposterous, satiric—a full spectrum.

HIS most important work, however, lies in the province of fantasy. In that field he was a bold and daring innovator, and his contributions to the central fantasy tradition (that of a story set in surroundings invented by the author) were permanent and left their mark on all fantasy written after his.

The major part of his work in fantasy is to be found in eight slender collections of short stories published between 1905, when his first volume, *The Gods of Pegāna,* appeared, and 1919, the date of *Tales of Three Hemispheres.* With the publication of that final collection of tales, Dunsany turned to other fields, such as the novel. But even then he was not finished with fantasy itself, for many of his novels are also in the genre he had opened up to new horizons and made his own. I refer to such enchanting and magical entertainments as *Don Rodriguez: Chronicles of Shadow Valley* (1922), *The King of Elfland's Daughter* (1924), *The Charwoman's Shadow* (1926), and *The Blessings of Pan* (1927).

When Lord Dunsany died in 1957 at the age of nearly eighty, he was succeeded by his son, the Honorable Randall Plunkett, who became the nineteenth baron. But no one has yet succeeded to his other title—that of the finest of all fantasy writers. And I do not think we shall see his equal in our time.

IN the pages of this book I have brought together twenty-five of his finest fantasy stories, as well as one major novella, or short novel. Also included are two of his most brilliant and fantastical plays, four of his short-short stories, and (just to give you a balanced and comprehensive view of his entire literary career) four of the later short stories concerning Mr. Joseph Jorkens, the world traveler and noted clubman. The earliest of the stories appeared in 1906, the latest in 1948. This third Dunsanian collection, therefore, spans more than forty years of Dunsany's life.

I have given it my own title: *Over the Hills and Far Away*. To me it evokes something of the elusive, haunting quality I find in the tales of Lord Dunsany. There is in them the glimmer of strange marvels in distant, fabulous realms; the equally beckoning glamor and mystery of unknown lands that lie just over the next hilltop, beyond the next horizon; a deep, almost mystical love for the earth itself as well; and a joyous celebration of the forces of nature.

I am also reminded of another quotation, however, very familiar, often repeated:

> *Unhappy far-off things*
> *And battles long ago . . .*

The words are from Wordsworth; but writer after writer has made them his own. You will find the first line used as a book title by Arthur Machen. Even Dunsany himself made it the title of one of his books! But Lord Dunsany writes of *happy* far-off things: there is only joy in him, little sorrow, and many miracles.

LIN CARTER
Editorial Consultant:
The Ballantine Adult Fantasy Series
Hollis, Long Island, New York

ON READING LORD DUNSANY'S "BOOK OF WONDER"

The hours of night unheeded fly,
   And in the grate the embers fade;
Vast shadows one by one pass by
   In silent daemon cavalcade.

But still the magic volume holds
   The raptur'd eye in realms apart,
And fulgent sorcery enfolds
   The willing mind and eager heart.

The lonely room no more is there—
   For to the sight in pomp appear
Temples and cities pois'd in air
   And blazing glories—sphere on sphere.

             H. P. LOVECRAFT

Over the Hills and Far Away

And I would love you all the day,
If with me you'd fondly stray
Over the hills and far away.

—JOHN GAY

Tales of the
World's Edge

Editor's Note

LORD DUNSANY'S first book, *The Gods of Pegāna*, introduced a fresh, original concept into modern fantasy literature. Here was an author seriously attempting the creation of an invented world. For that initial collection of fables and prose-poems told us of the myths and liturgies of the gods and goddesses of an imaginary milieu which he called "the little kingdoms at the World's Edge" or "in the Third Hemisphere." Successive collections of tales went on to relate the legends of the prophets, kings, and heroes who inhabited those shadowy realms at the World's Edge and prayed to those deities.

Collected here in the first part of *Over the Hills and Far Away* are the last few tales (left out of my first two Dunsany books) which are set in the little kingdoms at the World's Edge or in those realms contiguous to them. "The Journey of the King" has hitherto been passed over solely because of its length. (At about 13,200 words, it is really a novella, not a short story.) But it is too good to omit. And I did not include "The Fall of Babbulkund" in either of the two earlier collections because I had already previously reprinted it in *New Worlds for Old*. But as that anthology was published in 1971 and is now out of print, I feel the Babbulkund story should at last appear in one of these Dunsanian collections, where it really belongs.

As for "The Compromise of the King of the Golden Isles"—of course it is actually a play. But it is also such a gorgeous, magical piece of story-telling that it reads as splendidly as it acts. And since nobody seems to produce Dunsany's plays any more—there has not been one mounted for many years—you are not likely in any event to have the opportunity of seeing it on the stage.

L.C.

The Journey of the King

I

One day the King turned to the women that danced and said to them: "Dance no more," and those that bore the wine in jewelled cups he sent away. The palace of King Ebalon was emptied of sound of song and there rose the voices of heralds crying in the streets to find the prophets of the land.

Then went the dancers, the cupbearer and the singers down into the hard streets among the houses, Pattering Leaves, Silvern Fountain and Summer Lightning, the dancers whose feet the gods had not devised for stony ways, which had only danced for princes. And with them went the singer, Soul of the South, and the sweet singer, Dream of the Sea, whose voices the gods had attuned to the ears of kings, and old Istahn the cupbearer left his life's work in the palace to tread the common ways, he that had stood at the elbows of three kings of Zarkandhu and had watched his ancient vintage feeding their valour and mirth as the waters of Tondaris feed the green plains to the south. Ever he had stood grave among their jests, but his heart warmed itself solely by the fire of the mirth of kings. He too, with the singers and dancers, went out into the dark.

And throughout the land the heralds sought out the prophets thereof. Then one evening as King Ebalon sat alone within his palace there were brought before him all who had repute for wisdom and who wrote the histories of the times to be. Then the King spake, saying: "The King goeth upon a journey with many horses, yet riding upon none, when the pomp of travelling shall be heard in the streets and the sound of the lute and the drum and the name of the King. And I would know

5

what princes and what people shall greet me on the
other shore in the land to which I travel."

Then fell a hush upon the prophets for they murmured: "All knowledge is with the King."

Then said the King: "Thou first, Samahn, High
Prophet of the Temple of gold in Azinorn, answer or
thou shalt write no more the history of the times to be,
but shalt toil with thy hand to make record of the little
happenings of the days that were, as do the common
men."

Then said Samahn: "All knowledge is with the King,
and when the pomp of travelling shall be heard in the
streets and the slow horses whereon the King rideth not
go behind lute and drum, then, as the King well knoweth, thou shalt go down to the great white house of
Kings and, entering the portals where none are worthy
to follow, shalt make obeisance alone to all the elder
Kings of Zarkandhu, whose bones are seated upon
golden thrones grasping their sceptres still. Therein
thou shalt go with robes, and scepter through the
marble porch, but thou shalt leave behind thee thy
gleaming crown that others may wear it, and as the times
go by come in to swell the number of the thirty Kings
that sit in the great white house on golden thrones.
There is one doorway in the great white house, and
it stands wide with marble portals yawning for kings,
but when it shall receive thee, and thine obeisance hath
been made because of thine obligation to the thirty
Kings, thou shalt find at the back of the house an unknown door through which the soul of a King may just
pass, and leaving thy bones upon a golden throne thou
shalt go unseen out of the great white house to tread
the velvet spaces that lie among the worlds. Then, O
King, it were well to travel fast and not to tarry about
the houses of men as do the souls of some who still be-
wail the sudden murder that sent them upon the journey
before their time, and who, being yet loth to go, linger
in dark chambers all the night. These, setting forth to
travel in the dawn and travelling all the day, see earth

behind them gleaming when evening falls, and again are loth to leave its pleasant haunts, and come back again through dark woods and up into some old loved chamber, and ever tarry between home and flight and find no rest.

"Thou wilt set forth at once because the journey is far and lasts for many hours; but the hours on the velvet spaces are the hours of the gods, and we may not say what time such an hour may be if reckoned in mortal years.

"At last thou shalt come to a grey place filled with mist, with grey shapes standing before it which are altars, and on the altars rise small red flames from dying fires that scarce illumine the mist. And in the mist it is dark and cold because the fires are low. These are the altars of the people's faiths, and the flames are the worship of men, and through the mist the gods of Old go groping in the dark and in the cold. There thou shalt hear a voice cry feebly: 'Inyani, Inyani, lord of the thunder, where art thou, for I cannot see?' And a voice shall answer faintly in the cold: 'O maker of many worlds, I am here.' And in that place the gods of Old are nearly deaf for the prayers of men grow few, they are nigh blind because the fires burn low upon the altars of men's faiths and they are very cold. And all about the place of mist there lies a moaning sea which is called the Sea of Souls. And behind the place of mist are the dim shapes of mountains, and on the peak of one there glows a silvern light that shines in the moaning sea; and ever as the flames on the altars die before the gods of Old the light on the mountain increases, and the light shines over the mist and never through it as the gods of Old grow blind. It is said that the light on the mountain shall one day become a new god who is not of the gods of Old.

"There, O King, thou shalt enter the Sea of Souls by the shore where the altars stand which are covered in mist. In that sea are the souls of all that ever lived on the worlds and all that ever shall live, all freed from earth and flesh. And all the souls in that sea are aware of one another but more than with hearing or sight or by taste or touch or smell, and they all speak to each other yet not with lips, with voices which need no sound. And over the sea lies music as winds o'er an ocean on earth, and there unfettered by language great thoughts set outward through the souls as on earth the currents go.

"Once did I dream that in a mist-built ship I sailed upon that sea and heard the music that is not of instruments, and voices not from lips, and woke and found that I was upon the earth and that gods had lied to me in the night. Into this sea from fields of battle and cities come down the rivers of lives, and ever the gods have taken onyx cups and far and wide into the worlds again have flung the souls out of the sea, that each may find a prison in the body of a man with five small windows closely barred, and each one shackled with forgetfulness.

"But all the while the light on the mountain grows, and none may say what work the god that shall be born of the silvern light shall work on the Sea of Souls, when the gods of Old are dead and the Sea is living still."

And answer made the King:

"Thou that art a prophet of the gods of Old; go back and see that those red flames burn more brightly on the altars, in the mist, for the gods of Old are easy and pleasant gods, and thou canst not say what toil shall vex our souls when the god of the light on the mountain shall stride along the shore where bleach the huge bones of the gods of Old."

And Samahn answered: "All knowledge is with the King."

II

Then the King called to Ynath bidding him speak concerning the journey of the King. Ynath was the prophet that sat at the Eastern gate of the Temple of

Gorandhu. There Ynath prayed his prayers to all the passers by lest ever the gods should go abroad, and one should pass him dressed in a mortal guise. And men are pleased as they walk by that Eastern gate that Ynath should pray to them for fear that they be gods, so men bring gifts to Ynath in the Eastern gate.

And Ynath said: "All knowledge is with the King. When a strange ship comes to anchor in the air outside thy chamber window, thou shalt leave thy well-kept garden and it shall become a prey to the nights and days and be covered again with grass. But going aboard thou shalt set sail over the Sea of Time and well shall the ship steer through the many worlds and still sail on. If other ships shall pass thee on the way and hail thee saying: 'From what port?' thou shalt answer them: 'From Earth.' And if they ask thee 'Whither bound?' then thou shalt answer: 'The End.' Or thou shalt hail them saying, 'From what port?' And they shall answer: 'From The End called also The Beginning: and bound to Earth.' And thou shalt sail away till like an old sorrow dimly felt by happy men the worlds shall gleam in the distance like one star, and as the star pales thou shalt come to the shore of space where æons rolling shorewards from Time's sea shall lash up centuries to foam away in years. There lies the Centre Garden of the gods, facing full seawards. All around lie songs that on earth were never sung, fair thoughts not heard among the worlds, dream pictures never seen that drifted over Time without a home till at last the æons swept them on to the shore of space. And in the Centre Garden of the gods bloom many fancies. Therein once some souls were playing where the gods walked up and down and to and fro. And a dream came in more beauteous than the rest on the crest of a wave of Time, and one soul going downward to the shore clutched at the dream and caught it. Then over the dreams and stories and old songs that lay on the shore of space the hours came sweeping back, and the centuries caught that soul and swirled him with his dream far out to the Sea of Time,

and the æons swept him earthwards and cast him into
a palace with all the might of the sea and left him there
with his dream. The child grew to a King and still
clutched at his dream till the people wondered and
laughed. Then, O King, Thou didst cast thy dream back
into the Sea, and Time drowned it and men laughed no
more, but thou didst forget that a certain sea beat on
a distant shore and that there was a garden and therein
souls. But at the end of the journey that thou shalt take,
when thou comest to the shore of space again thou
shalt go up the beach, and coming to a garden gate
that stands in a garden wall shalt remember these things
again, for it stands where the hours assail not above
the beating of Time, far up the shore, and nothing alter-
eth there. So thou shalt go through the garden gate and
hear again the whispering of the souls when they talk
low where sing the voices of the gods. There with kindred souls thou shalt speak as thou didst of yore and
tell them what befell thee beyond the tides of time and
how they took thee and made of thee a King so that thy
soul found no rest. There in the Centre Garden thou
shalt sit at ease and watch the gods all rainbow-clad
go up and down and to and fro on the paths of dreams
and songs, and shalt not venture down to the cheerless
sea. For that which a man loves most is not on this side
of Time, and all which drifts on its æons is a lure.

"All knowledge is with the King."

Then said the King: "Ay, there was a dream once
but Time hath swept it away."

III

Then spake Monith, Prophet of the Temple of Azure
that stands on the snow-peak of Ahmoon and said: "All
knowledge is with the King. Once thou didst set out
upon a one day's journey riding upon thy horse and
before thee had gone a beggar down the road, and his
name was Yeb. Him thou didst overtake and when he
heeded not thy coming thou didst ride over him.

"Upon the journey that thou shalt one day take riding upon no horse, this beggar has set out before thee and is labouring up the crystal steps towards the moon as a man goeth up the steps of a high tower in the dark. On the moon's edge beneath the shadow of Mount Angises he shall rest awhile and then shall climb the crystal steps again. Then a great journey lies before him before he may rest again till he come to that star that is called the left eye of Gundo. Then a journey of many crystal steps lieth before him again with nought to guide him but the light of Omrazu. On the edge of Omrazu shall Yeb tarry long, for the most dreadful part of his journey lieth before him. Up the crystal steps that lie beyond Omrazu he must go, and any that follow, through the howling of all the meteors that ride the sky; for in that part of the crystal space go many meteors up and down all squealing in the dark, which greatly perplex all travellers. And, if he may see through the gleaming of the meteors and in spite of their uproar come safely through, he shall come to the star Omrund at the edge of the Track of Stars. And from star to star along the Track of Stars the soul of a man may travel with more ease, and there the journey lies no more straight forward, but curves to the right."

Then said King Ebalon:

"Of this beggar whom my horse smote down thou hast spoken much, but I sought to know by what road a King should go when he taketh his last royal journey, and what princes and what people should meet him upon another shore."

Then answered Monith:

"All knowledge is with the King. It hath been doomed by the gods, who speak not in jest, that thou shalt follow the soul that thou didst send alone upon its journey, that that soul go not unattended up the crystal steps.

"Moreover, as this beggar went upon his lonely journey he dared to curse the King, and his curses lie like a red mist along the valleys and hollows wherever he uttered them. By these red mists, O King, thou shalt fare at last to the land wherein he hath blessed thee (repenting of anger at last), and thou shalt see his blessing lie over the land like a blaze of golden sunshine illumining fields and gardens."

Then said the King:

"The gods have spoken hard above the snowy peak of this mountain Ahmoon."

And Monith said:

"How a man may come to the shore of space beyond the tides of time I know not, but it is doomed that thou shalt certainly first follow the beggar past the moon, Omrund and Omrazu till thou comest to the Track of Stars, and up the Track of Stars coming towards the right along the edge of it till thou comest to Ingazi. There the soul of the beggar Yeb sat long, then, breathing deep, set off on his great journey earthward adown the crystal steps. Straight through the spaces where no stars are found to rest at, following the dull gleam of earth and her fields till he come at last where journeys end and start."

Then said King Ebalon:

"If this hard tale be true, how shall I find the beggar that I must follow when I come again to the earth?"

And the Prophet answered:

"Thou shalt know him by his name and find him in this place, for that beggar shall be called King Ebalon and he shall be sitting upon the throne of the Kings of Zarkandhu."

And the King answered:

"If one sit upon this throne whom men call King Ebalon, who then shall I be?"

And the Prophet answered:

"Thou shalt be a beggar and thy name shall be Yeb, and thou shalt ever tread the road before the palace waiting for alms from the King whom men shall call Ebalon."

Then said the King:

"Hard gods indeed are those that tramp the snows

of Ahmoon about the Temple of Azure, for if I sinned against this beggar called Yeb, they too have sinned against him when they doomed him to travel on this weary journey though he hath not offended."

And Monith said:

"He too hath offended, for he was angry as thy horse struck him, and the gods smite anger. And his anger and his curses doom him to journey without rest as also they doom thee."

Then said the King:

"Thou that sittest upon Ahmoon in the Temple of Azure, dreaming thy dreams and making prophecies, foresee the ending of this weary quest and tell me where it shall be?"

And Monith answered:

"As a man looks across great lakes I have gazed into the days to be, and as the great flies come upon four wings of gauze to skim over blue waters, so have my dreams come sailing two by two out of the days to be. And I dreamed that that King Ebalon, whose soul was not thy soul, stood in his palace in a time far hence, and beggars thronged the street outside, and among them was Yeb, a beggar, having thy soul. And it was on the morning of a festival and the King came robed in white, with all his prophets and his seers and magicians, all down the marble steps to bless the land and all that stood therein as far as the purple hills, because it was the morning of a festival. And as the King raised up his hand over the beggars' heads to bless the fields and rivers and all that stood therein, I dreamed that the quest was ended.

"All knowledge is with the King."

IV

Evening darkened and above the palace domes gleamed out the stars whereon haply others missed the secret too.

And outside the palace in the dark they that had borne the wine in jewelled cups mocked in low voices at the King and at the wisdom of his prophets.

Then spake Ynar, called the prophet of the Crystal Peak; for there rises Amanath above all that land, a mountain whose peak is crystal, and Ynar beneath its summit hath his Temple, and when day shines no longer on the world Amanath takes the sunlight and gleams afar as a beacon in a bleak land lit at night. And at the hour when all faces are turned on Amanath, Ynar comes forth beneath the Crystal Peak to weave strange spells and to make signs that people say are surely for the gods. Therefore it is said in all those lands that Ynar speaks at evening to the gods when all the world is still.

And Ynar said:

"All knowledge is with the King, and without doubt it hath come to the King's ears how certain speech is held at evening on the Peak of Amanath.

"They that speak to me at evening on the Peak are They that live in a city through whose streets Death walketh not, and I have heard it from Their Elders that the King shall take no journey; only from thee the hills shall slip away, the dark woods, the sky and all the gleaming worlds that fill the night, and the green fields shall go on untrodden by thy feet and the blue sky ungazed at by thine eyes, and still the rivers shall all run seaward but making no music in thine ears. And all the old laments shall still be spoken, troubling thee not, and to the earth shall fall the tears of the children of earth and never grieving thee. Pestilence, heat and cold, ignorance, famine and anger, these things shall grip their claws upon all men as heretofore in fields and roads and cities but shall not hold thee. But from thy soul, sitting in the old worn track of the worlds when all is gone away, shall fall off the shackles of circumstances and thou shalt dream thy dreams alone.

"And thou shalt find that dreams are real where there

is nought as far as the Rim but only thy dreams and thee.

"With them thou shalt build palaces and cities resting upon nothing and having no place in time, not to be assailed by the hours or harmed by ivy or rust, not to be taken by conquerors, but destroyed by thy fancy if thou dost wish it so or by thy fancy rebuilded. And nought shall ever disturb these dreams of thine which here are troubled and lost by all the happenings of earth, as the dreams of one who sleeps in a tumultous city. For these thy dreams shall sweep outward like a strong river over a great waste plain wherein are neither rocks nor hills to turn it, only in that place there shall be no boundaries nor sea, neither hindrance nor end. And it were well for thee that thou shouldst take few regrets into thy waste dominions from the world where-in thou livest, for such regrets or any memory of deeds ill done must sit beside thy soul for ever in that waste, singing one song always of forlorn remorse; and they too shall be only dreams but very real.

"There nought shall hinder thee among thy dreams, for even the gods may harass thee no more when flesh and earth and events with which They bound thee shall have slipped away."

Then said the King:

"I like not this grey doom, for dreams are empty. I would see action roaring through the world, and men and deeds."

Then answered the prophet:

"Victory, jewels and dancing but please thy fancy. What is the sparkle of the gem to thee without thy fancy which it allures, and thy fancy is all a dream. Action and deeds and men are nought without dreams and do but fetter them, and only dreams are real, and where thou stayest when the worlds shall drift away there shall be only dreams."

And the King answered:

"A mad prophet."

And Ynar said:

"A mad prophet, but believing that his soul possesseth all things of which his soul may become aware and that he is master of that soul, and thou a high-minded King believing only that thy soul possesseth such few countries as are leaguered by thine armies and the sea, and that thy soul is possessed by certain strange gods of whom thou knowest not, who shall deal with it in a way whereof thou knowest not. Until a knowledge come to us that either is wrong I have wider realms, O King, than thee and hold them beneath no overlords."

Then said the King:

"Thou hast said no overlords! To whom then dost thou speak by strange signs at evening above the world?"

And Ynar went forward a few paces and whispered to the King. And the King shouted:

"Seize ye this prophet for he is a hypocrite and speaks to no gods at evening above the world, but has deceived us with his signs."

And Ynar said:

"Come not near me or I shall point towards you when I speak at evening upon the mountain with Those that ye know of."

Then Ynar went away and the guards touched him not.

V

Then spake the prophet Thum, who was clad in seaweed and had no Temple, but lived apart from men. All his life he had lived on a lonely beach and had heard for ever the wailing of the sea and the crying of the wind in hollows among the cliffs. Some said that having lived so long by the full beating of the sea, and where always the wind cries loudest, he could not feel the joys of other men, but only felt the sorrow of the sea crying in his soul for ever.

"Long ago on the path of stars, midmost between the

worlds, there strode the gods of Old. In the bleak middle of the worlds They sat and the worlds went round and round, like dead leaves in the wind at Autumn's end, with never a life on one, while the gods went sighing for the things that might not be. And the centuries went over the gods to go where the centuries go, toward the End of Things, and with Them went the sighs of all the gods as They longed for what might not be.

"One by one in the midst of the worlds, fell dead the gods of Old, still sighing for the things that might not be, all slain by Their own regrets. Only Shimono Káni, the youngest of the gods, made him a harp out of the heart strings of all the elder gods, and sitting upon the Path of Stars all in the Midst of Things, played upon the harp a dirge for the gods of Old. And the song told of all vain regrets and of unhappy loves of the gods in the olden time, and of Their great deeds that were to adorn the future years. But into the dirge of Shimono Káni came voices crying out of the heart strings of the gods, all sighing still for the things that might not be. And the dirge and the voices crying, go drifting away from the Path of Stars, away from the Midst of Things, till they came twittering among the Worlds, like a great host of birds that are lost by night. And every note is a life, and many notes become caught up among the worlds to be entangled with flesh for a little while before they pass again on their journey to the great Anthem that roars at the End of Time. Shimono Káni hath given a voice to the wind and added a sorrow to the sea. But when in lighted chambers after feasting there arises the voice of the singer to please the King, then is the soul of that singer crying aloud to his fellows from where he stands chained to earth. And when at the sound of the singing the heart of the King grows sad and his princes lament then they remember, though knowing not that they remember it, the sad face of Shimono Káni sitting by his dead brethren, the elder gods, playing on that harp of crying heart strings whereby he sent their souls among the worlds.

"And when the music of one lute is lonely on the hills at night, then one soul calleth to his brother souls—the notes of Shimono Káni's dirge which have not been caught among the worlds—and he knoweth not to whom he calls or why, but knoweth only that minstrelsy is his only cry and sendeth it out into the dark.

"But although in the prison houses of earth all memories must die, yet as there sometimes clings to a prisoner's feet some dust of the fields wherein he was captured, so sometimes fragments of remembrance cling to a man's soul after it hath been taken to earth. Then a great minstrel arises, and, weaving together the shreds of his memories, maketh some melody such as the hand of Shimono Káni smites out of his harp; and they that pass by say: 'Hath there not been some such melody before?' and pass on sad at heart for memories which are not.

"Therefore, O King, one day the great gates of thy palace shall lie open for a procession wherein the King comes down to pass through a people, lamenting with lute and drum; and on the same day a prison door shall be opened by relenting hands, and one more lost note of Shimono Káni's dirge shall go back to swell his melody again.

"The dirge of Shimono Káni shall roll on till one day it shall come with all its notes complete to overwhelm the Silence that sits at the End of Things. Then shall Shimono Káni say to his brethren's bones: 'The things that might not be have at last become.'

"But very quiet shall be the bones of the gods of Old and only Their voices shall live which cried from the harp of heart strings, for the things which might not be."

VI

When the caravans, saying farewell to Zandara, set out across the waste northwards toward Einandhu, they follow the desert track for seven days before they come to water where Shubah Onath rises black out of the waste, with a well at its foot and herbage on its summit. On this rock a prophet hath his Temple and is called the Prophet of Journeys, and hath carven in a southern window smiling along the camel track all gods that are benignant to caravans.

There a traveller may learn by prophecy whether he shall accomplish the ten days' journey thence across the desert and so come to the white city of Einandhu, or whether his bones shall lie with the bones of old along the desert track.

No name hath the Prophet of Journeys, for none is needed in that desert where no man calls nor ever a man answers.

Thus spake the Prophet of Journeys standing before the King:

"The journey of the King shall be an old journey pushed on apace.

"Many a year before the making of the moon thou camest down with dream camels from the City without a name that stands beyond all the stars. And then began thy journey over the Waste of Nought, and thy dream camel bore thee well when those of certain of thy fellow travellers fell down in the Waste and were covered over by the silence and were turned again to nought; and those travellers when their dream camels fell, having nothing to carry them further over the Waste, were lost beyond and never found the earth. These are those men that might have been but were not. And all about thee fluttered the myraid hours travelling in great swarms across the Waste of Nought.

"How many centuries passed across the cities while thou wast making thy journey none may reckon, for there is no time in the Waste of Nought, but only the hours fluttering earthwards from beyond to do the work of Time. At last the dream-borne travellers saw far off a green place gleaming and made haste towards it and so came to Earth. And there, O King, ye rest for a little while, thou and those that came with thee, making an encampment upon earth before journeying on. There the swarming hours alight, settling on every blade of grass and tree, and spreading over your tents and devouring all things, and at last bending your very tent poles with their weight and wearying you.

"Behind the encampment in the shadow of the tents lurks a dark figure with a nimble sword, having the name of Time. This is he that hath called the hours from beyond and he it is that is their master, and it is his work that the hours do as they devour all green things upon the earth and tatter the tents and weary all the travellers. As each of the hours does the work of Time, Time smites him with his nimble sword as soon as his work is done, and the hour falls severed to the dust with his bright wings scattered, as a locust cut asunder by the scimitar of a skillful swordsman.

"One by one, O King, with a stir in the camp, and the folding up of the tents one by one, the travellers shall push on again on the journey begun so long before out of the City without a name to the place where dream camels go, striding free through the Waste. So into the Waste, O King, thou shalt set forth ere long, perhaps to renew friendships begun during thy short encampment upon earth.

"Other green places thou shalt meet in the Waste and thereon shalt encamp again until driven thence by the hours. What prophet shall relate how many journeys thou shalt make or how many encampments? But at last thou shalt come to the place of The Resting of Camels, and there shall gleaming cliffs that are named The Ending of Journeys lift up out of the Waste of Nought, Nought at their feet, Nought lying wide before them, with only the glint of worlds far off to illumine the Waste. One by one, on tired dream camels, the travellers shall come in, and going up the pathway through the cliff in that land of The Resting of Camels shall come on The City of Ceasing. There, the dream-wrought pinnacles and the spires that are builded of men's hopes shall rise up real before thee, seen only hitherto as a mirage in the Waste.

"So far the swarming hours may not come, and far away among the tents shall stand the dark figure with the nimble sword. But in the scintillant streets, under the song-built abodes of the last of cities, thy journey, O King, shall end."

VII

In the valley beyond Sidono there lies a garden of poppies, and where the poppies' heads are all a-swing with summer breezes that go up the valley there lies a path well strewn with ocean shells. Over Sidono's summit the birds come streaming to the lake that lies in the valley of the garden, and behind them rises the sun sending Sidono's shadow as far as the edge of the lake. And down the path of many ocean shells when they begin to gleam in the sun, every morning walks an aged man clad in a silken robe with strange devices woven. A little temple where the old man lives stands at the edge of the path. None worship there, for Zornadhu, the old prophet, hath forsaken men to walk among his poppies.

For Zornadhu hath failed to understand the purport of Kings and cities and the moving up and down of many people to the tune of the clinking of gold. Therefore hath Zornadhu gone far away from the sound of cities and from those that are ensnared thereby, and beyond Sidono's mountain and hath come to rest where there are neither kings nor armies nor bartering for gold, but only the heads of the poppies that sway in the wind together and the birds that fly from Sidono to the lake, and then the sunrise over Sidono's summit; and afterwards the flight of birds out of the lake and over Sidono again, and sunset behind the valley, and high over lake and garden the stars that know not cities. There Zornadhu lives in his garden of poppies with Sidono standing between him and the whole world of men; and when the wind blowing athwart the valley sways the heads of the tall poppies against the Temple wall, the old prophet says: "The flowers are all praying, and lo! they be nearer to the gods than men."

But the heralds of the King coming after many days of travel to the crest of Sidono perceived the garden valley. By the lake they saw the poppy garden gleaming round and small like a sunrise over water on a misty morning seen by some shepherd from the hills. And descending the bare mountain for three days they came to the gaunt pines, and ever between the tall trunks came the glare of the poppies that shone from the garden valley. For a whole day they travelled through the pines. That night a cold wind came up the garden valley crying against poppies. Low in his Temple, with a song of exceeding grief, Zornadhu in the morning made a dirge for the passing of poppies, because in the night time there had fallen petals that might not return or ever come again into the garden valley. Outside the Temple on the path of ocean shells the heralds halted, and read the names and honours of the King; and from the Temple came the voice of Zornadhu still singing his lament. But they took him from his garden because of the King's command, and down his gleaming path of ocean shells and away up Sidono, and left the Temple empty with none to lament when silken poppies died. And the will of the wind of the autumn was wrought upon the poppies, and the heads of the poppies that rose from the earth went down to the earth again, as the plume of a warrior smitten in a heathen fight far away, where there are none to lament him. Thus out of his land of flowers went Zornadhu and came perforce into the lands of men, and saw cities, and in the city's midst stood up before the King.

And the King said:

"Zornadhu, what of the journey of the King and of the princes and the people that shall meet me?"

Zornadhu answered:

"I know nought of Kings, but in the night time the

poppy made his journey a little before dawn. There-after the wild-fowl came as is their wont over Sidono's summit, and the sun rising behind them gleamed upon Sidono, and all the flowers of the lake awoke. And the bee passing up and down the garden went droning to other poppies, and the flowers of the lake, they that had known the poppy, knew him no more. And the sun's rays slanting from Sidono's crest lit still a garden valley where one poppy waved his petals to the dawn no more. And I, O King, that down a path of gleaming ocean shells walk in the morning, found not, nor have since found, that poppy again, that hath gone on the journey whence there is not returning, out of my garden valley. And I, O King, made a dirge to cry beyond that valley and the poppies bowed their heads; but there is no cry nor no lament that may adjure the life to return again to a flower that grew in a garden once and hereafter is not.

"Unto what place the lives of poppies have gone no man shall truly say. Sure it is that to that place are only outward tracks. Only it may be that when a man dreams at evening in a garden where heavily the scent of poppies hangs in the air, when the winds have sunk, and far away the sound of a lute is heard on lonely hills, as he dreams of silken-scarlet poppies that once were a-swing together in the gardens of his youth, the lives of those old lost poppies shall return, living again in his dream. *So there may dream the gods*. And through the dreams of some divinity reclining in tinted fields above the morning we may haply pass again, although our bodies have long swirled up and down the world with other dust. In these strange dreams our lives may be again, all in the centre of our hopes, rejoicings and laments, until above the morning the gods wake to go about their work, haply to remember still Their idle dreams, haply to dream them all again in the stillness when shines the starlight of the gods."

VIII

Then said the King: "I like not these strange journeys nor this faint wandering through the dreams of gods like the shadow of a weary camel that may not rest when the sun is low. The gods that have made me to love the earth's cool woods and dancing streams do ill to send me into the starry spaces that I love not, with my soul still peering earthward through the eternal years, as a beggar who once was noble staring from the street at lighted halls. For wherever the gods may send me I shall be, as the gods have made me, a creature loving the green fields of earth.

"Now if there stand one prophet here that hath the ear of those too splendid gods that stride above the glories of the orient sky, tell them that there is on earth one King in the land called Zarkandhu to the south of the opal mountains, who would fain tarry among the many gardens of earth, and would leave to other men the splendours that the gods shall give the dead above the twilight that surrounds the stars."

Then spake Yamen, prophet of the Temple of Obin that stands on the shores of a great lake, facing east. Yamen said: "I pray oft to the gods who sit above the twilight behind the east. When the clouds are heavy and red at sunset, or when there is boding of thunder or eclipse, then I pray not, lest my prayers be scattered and beaten earthward. But when the sun sets in a tranquil sky, pale green or azure, and the light of his farewells stays long upon lonely hills, then I send forth my prayers to flutter upward to gods that are surely smiling, and the gods hear my prayers. But, O King, boons sought out of due time from the gods are never wholly to be desired, and, if They should grant to thee to tarry on the earth, old age would trouble thee with burdens more and more till thou wouldst become the driven slave of the hours in fetters that none may break."

The King said: "They that have devised this burden

of age may surely stay it; pray therefore on the calmest evening of the year to the gods above the twilight that I may tarry always on the earth and always young, while over my head the scourges of the gods pass and alight not."

Then answered Yamen: "The King hath commanded, yet among the blessings of the gods there always cries a curse. The great princes that make merry with the King, who tell of the great deeds that the King wrought in the former time, shall one by one grow old. And thou, O King, seated at the feast crying, 'make merry' and extolling the former time shall find about thee white heads nodding in sleep, and men that are forgetting the former time. Then one by one the names of those that sported with thee once called by the gods, one by one the names of the singers that sing the songs thou lovest called by the gods, lastly of those that chased the grey boar by night and took him in Orghoom river—only the King. Then a new people that have not known the old deeds of the King nor fought and chased with him, who dare not make merry with the King as did his long dead princes. And all the while those princes that are dead growing dearer and greater in thy memory, and all the while the men that served thee then growing more small to thee. And all the old things fading and new things arising which are not as the old things were, the world changing yearly before thine eyes and the gardens of thy childhood overgrown. Because thy childhood was in the olden years thou shalt love the olden years, but ever the new years shall overthrow them and their customs, and not the will of a King may stay the changes that the gods have planned for all of the customs of old. Ever thou shalt say 'This was not so,' and ever the new custom shall prevail even against a King. When thou hast made merry a thousand times thou shalt grow tired of making merry. At last thou shalt become weary of the chase, and still old age shall not come near to thee to stifle desires that have been too oft fulfilled; then, O King, thou shalt be a hunter yearning for the chase but with nought to pursue that hath not been oft overcome. Old age shall come not to bury thine ambitions in a time when there is nought for thee to aspire to any more. Experience of many centuries shall make thee wise but hard and very sad, and thou shalt be a mind apart from thy fellows and curse them all for fools, and they shall not perceive thy wisdom because thy thoughts are not their thoughts and the gods that they have made are not the gods of the olden time. No solace shall thy wisdom bring thee but only an increasing knowledge that thou knowest nought, and thou shalt feel as a wise man in a world of fools, or else as a fool in a world of wise men, when all men feel so sure and ever thy doubts increase. When all that spake with thee of thine old deeds are dead, those that saw them not shall speak of them again to thee; till one speaking to thee of thy deeds of valour add more than even a man should when speaking to a King, and thou shalt suddenly doubt whether these great deeds were; and there shall be none to tell thee, only the echoes of the voices of the gods still singing in thine ears when long ago They called the princes that were thy friends. And thou shalt hear the knowledge of the olden time most wrongly told and afterwards forgotten. Then many prophets shall arise claiming discovery of that old knowledge. Then thou shalt find that seeking knowledge is vain, as the chase is vain, as making merry is vain, as all things are vain. One day thou shalt find that it is vain to be a King. Greatly then will the acclamations of the people weary thee, till the time when people grow aweary of Kings. Then thou shalt know that thou hast been uprooted from thine olden time and set to live in uncongenial years, and jests all new to royal ears shall smite thee on the head like hailstones, when thou hast lost thy crown, when those to whose grandsires thou hadst granted to bring them as children to kiss the feet of the King shall mock at thee because thou hast not learnt to barter with gold.

"Not all the marvels of the future time shall atone

to thee for those old memories that glow warmer and brighter every year as they recede into the ages that the gods have gathered. And always dreaming of thy long dead princes and of the great Kings of other kingdoms in the olden time thou shalt fail to see the grandeur to which a hurrying jesting people shall attain in that kingless age. Lastly, O King, thou shalt perceive men changing in a way thou shalt not comprehend, knowing what thou canst not know, till thou shalt discover that these are men no more and a new race holds dominion over the earth whose forefathers were men. These shall speak to thee no more as they hurry upon a quest that thou shalt never understand, and thou shalt know that thou canst no longer take part in shaping destinies, but in a world of cities shall only pine for air and the waving grass again, and the sound of a wind in trees. Then even this shall end with the shapes of the gods in the darkness gathering all lives but thine, when the hills shall fling up earth's long stored heat back to the heavens again, when earth shall be old and cold, with nothing alive upon it but one King."

Then said the King:

"Pray to those hard gods still, for those that have loved the earth with all its gardens and woods and singing streams will love earth still when it is old and cold with all its gardens gone and all the purport of its being failed and nought but memories."

IX

Then spake Paharn, a prophet of the land of Hurn.

And Paharn said:

"There was one man that knew, but he stands not here."

And the King said:

"Is he further than my heralds might travel in the night if they went upon fleet horses?"

And the prophet answered:

"He is no further than thy heralds may well travel

in the night, but further than they may return from in all the years. Out of this city there goes a valley wandering through all the world and opens out at last on the green land of Hurn. On the one side in the distance gleams the sea, and on the other side a forest, black and ancient, darkens the fields of Hurn; beyond the forest and the sea there is no more, saving the twilight and beyond that the gods. In the mouth of the valley sleeps the village of Rhistaun.

"Here I was born, and heard the murmur of the flocks and herds, and saw the tall smoke standing between the sky and the still roofs of Rhistaun, and learned that men might not go into the dark forest, and that beyond the forest and the sea was nought saving the twilight, and beyond that the gods. Often there came travellers from the world all down the winding valley, and spake with strange speech in Rhistaun and returned again up the valley going back to the world. Sometimes with bells and camels and men running on foot, Kings came down the valley from the world, but always the travellers returned by the valley again and none went further than the land of Hurn.

"And Kithneb also was born in the land of Hurn and tended the flocks with me, but Kithneb would not care to listen to the murmur of the flocks and herds and see the tall smoke standing between the roofs and the sky, but needed to know how far from Hurn it was that the world met the twilight, and how far across the twilight sat the gods.

"And often Kithneb dreamed as he tended the flocks and herds, and when others slept he would wander near to the edge of the forest wherein men might not go. And the elders of the land of Hurn reproved Kithneb when he dreamed; yet Kithneb was still as other men and mingled with his fellows until the day of which I will tell thee, O King. For Kithneb was aged about a score of years, and he and I were sitting near the flocks, and he gazed long at the point where the dark forest met the sea at the end of the land of Hurn. But when night drove the twilight down under the forest we brought the flocks together to Rhistaun, and I went up the street between the houses to see four princes that had come down the valley from the world, and they were clad in blue and scarlet and wore plumes upon their heads, and they gave us in exchange for our sheep some gleaming stones which they told us were of great value on the word of princes. And I sold them three sheep, and Darniag sold them eight.

"But Kithneb came not with the others to the market place where the four princes stood, but went alone across the fields to the edge of the forest.

"And it was upon the next morning that the strange thing befell Kithneb; for I saw him in the morning coming from the fields, and I hailed him with the shepherd's cry wherewith we shepherds call to one another, and he answered not. Then I stopped and spake to him, and Kithneb said not a word till I became angry and left him.

"Then we spake together concerning Kithneb, and others had hailed him, and he had not answered them, but to one he had said that he had heard the voices of the gods speaking beyond the forest and so would never listen more to the voices of men.

"Then we said: 'Kithneb is mad,' and none hindered him.

"Another took his place among the flocks, and Kithneb sat in the evenings by the edge of the forest on the plain, alone.

"So Kithneb spake to none for many days, but when any forced him to speak he said that every evening he heard the gods when they came to sit in the forest from over the twilight and sea, and that he would speak no more with men.

"But as the months went by, men in Rhistaun came to look on Kithneb as a prophet, and we were wont to point to him when strangers came down the valley from the world, saying:

" 'Here in the land of Hurn we have a prophet such

as you have not among your cities, for he speaks at evening with the gods.'

"A year had passed over the silence of Kithneb when he came to me and spake. And I bowed before him because we believed that he spake among the gods. And Kithneb said:

" 'I will speak to thee before the end because I am most lonely. For how may I speak again with men and women in the little streets of Rhistaun among the houses, when I have heard the voices of the gods singing above the twilight? But I am more lonely than ever Rhistaun wots of, for this I tell thee, *when I hear the gods I know not what They say*. Well indeed I know the voice of each, for ever calling me away from contentment; well I know Their voices as they call to my soul and trouble it; I know by Their tone when They rejoice, and I know when They are sad, for even the gods feel sadness. I know when over fallen cities of the past, and the curved white bones of heroes They sing the dirges of the gods' lament. But alas! Their words I know not, and the wonderful strains of the melody of Their speech beat on my soul and pass away unknown.

" 'Therefore I travelled from the land of Hurn till I came to the house of the prophet Arnin-Yo, and told him that I sought to find the meaning of the gods; and Arnin-Yo told me to ask the shepherds concerning all the gods, for what the shepherds knew it was meet for a man to know, and beyond that, knowledge turned into trouble.

" 'But I told Arnin-Yo that I had heard myself the voices of the gods and I knew that They were there beyond the twilight and so could never more bow down to the gods that the shepherds made from the red clay which they scooped with their hands out of the hillside.

" 'Then said Arnin-Yo to me:

" 'Natheless forget that thou hast heard the gods and bow down again to the gods of the red clay that the shepherds make, and find thereby the ease that the shepherds find, and at last die, remembering devoutly the gods of the red clay that the shepherds scooped with their hands out of the hill. For the gifts of the gods that sit beyond the twilight and smile at the gods of clay, are neither ease nor contentment."

" 'And I said:

" ' "The god that my mother made out of the red clay that she had got from the hill, fashioning it with many arms and eyes as she sang me songs of its power, and told me stories of its mystic birth, this god is lost and broken; and ever in my ears is ringing the melody of the gods."

" 'And Arnin-Yo said:

" ' "If thou wouldst still seek knowledge know that only those that come behind the gods may clearly know their meaning. And this thou canst only do by taking ship and putting out to sea from the land of Hurn and sailing up from the coast towards the forest. There the sea cliffs turn to the left or southward, and full upon them beats the twilight from over the sea, and there thou mayest come round behind the forest. Here where the world's edge mingles with the twilight the gods come in the evening, and if thou canst come behind Them thou shalt hear Their voices, clear beating full seaward and filling all the twilight with sound of song, and thou shalt know the meaning of the gods. But where the cliffs turn southward there sits behind the gods Brimdono, the oldest whirlpool in the sea, roaring to guard his masters. Him the gods have chained for ever to the floor of the twilit sea to guard the door of the forest that lieth above the cliffs. Here, then, if thou canst hear the voices of the gods as thou hast said, thou wilt know their meaning clear, but this will profit thee little when Brimdono drags thee down and all thy ship." '

"Thus spake Kithneb to me."

"But I said:

" 'O Kithneb, forget those whirlpool-guarded gods beyond the forest, and if thy small god be lost thou shalt worship with me the small god that my mother made. Thousands of years ago he conquered cities but it is not any longer an angry god. Pray to him, Kithneb, and he shall bring thee comfort and increase to thy flocks and a mild spring, and at the last a quiet ending for thy days.'

"But Kithneb heeded not, and only bade me find a fisher ship and men to row it. So on the next day we put forth from the land of Hurn in a boat that the fisher folk use. And with us came four of the fisher folk who rowed the boat while I held the rudder, but Kithneb sat and spake not in the prow. And we rowed westward up the coast till we came at evening where the cliffs turned southward and the twilight gleamed upon them and the sea.

"There we turned southwards and saw at once Brimdono. And as a man tears the purple cloak of a king slain in battle to divide it with other warriors,—Brimdono tore the sea. And ever around and around him with a gnarled hand Brimdono whirled the sail of some adventurous ship, the trophy of some calamity wrought in his greed for shipwreck long ago where he sat to guard his masters from all who fare on the sea. And ever one far-reaching empty hand swung up and down so that we durst go no nearer.

"Only Kithneb neither saw Brimdono nor heard his roar, and when we would go no further he bade us lower a small boat with oars out of the ship. Into this boat Kithneb descended, not heeding words from us, and onward rowed alone. A cry of triumph over ships and men Brimdono uttered before him, but Kithneb's eyes were turned toward the forest as he came up behind the gods. Upon his face the twilight beat full from the haunts of evening to illumine the smiles that grew about his eyes as he came behind the gods. Him that had found the gods above Their twilit cliffs, him that had heard Their voices close at last and knew their meaning clear, him, from the cheerless world with its doubtings and prophets that lie, from all hidden meanings, where the truth rang clear at last, Brimdono took."

But when Paharn ceased to speak, in the King's ears

the roar of Brimdono exulting over ancient triumphs and the whelming of ships seemed still to ring.

X

Then Mohontis spake, the hermit prophet, who lived in the deep untravelled woods that seclude Lake Ilana.

"I dreamed that to the west of all the seas I saw by vision the mouth of Munra-O, guarded by golden gates, and through the bars of the gates that guard the mysterious river of Munra-O I saw the flashes of golden barques, wherein the gods went up and down, and to and fro through the evening dusk. And I saw that Munra-O was a river of dreams such as came through remembered gardens in the night, to charm our infancy as we slept beneath the sloping gables of the houses of long ago. And Munra-O rolled down her dreams from the unknown inner land and slid them under the golden gates and out into the waste, unheeding sea, till they beat far off upon low-lying shores and murmured songs of long ago to the islands of the south, or shouted tumultuous pæans to the Northern crags; or cried forlornly against rocks where no one came, dreams that might not be dreamed.

"Many gods there be, that through the dusk of an evening in the summer go up and down this river. There I saw, in a high barque all of gold, gods of the pomp of cities; there I saw gods of splendour, in boats bejewelled to the keels; gods of magnificence and gods of power. I saw the dark ships and the glint of steel of the gods whose trade was war, and I heard the melody of the bells of silver arow in the rigging of harpstrings as the gods of melody went sailing through the dusk on the river of Munra-O. Wonderful river of Munra-O! I saw a grey ship with sails of the spider's web all lit with dewdrop lanterns, and on its prow was a scarlet cock with its wings spread far and wide when the gods of the dawn sailed also on Munra-O.

"Down this river it is the wont of the gods to carry the

souls of men eastward to where the world in the distance faces on Munra-O. Then I knew that when the gods of the Pride of Power and gods of the Pomp of Cities went down the river in their tall gold ships to take earthward other souls, swiftly adown the river and between the ships had gone in his boat of birch bark the god Tarn, the hunter, bearing my soul to the world. And I know now that he came down the stream in the dusk keeping well to the middle, and that he moved silently and swiftly among the ships, wielding a twin-bladed oar. I remember, now, the yellow gleaming of the great boats of the gods of the Pomp of Cities, and the huge prow above me of the gods of the Pride of Power, when Tarn, dipping his right blade into the river, lifted his left blade high, and the drops gleamed and fell. Thus Tarn the hunter took me to the world that faces across the sea of the west on the gate of Munra-O. And so it was that there grew upon me the glamour of the hunt, though I had forgotten Tarn, and took me into mossy places and into dark woods, and I became the cousin of the wolf and looked in the lynx's eyes and knew the bear; and the birds called to me with half-remembered notes, and there grew in me a deep love of great rivers and of all western seas, and a distrust of cities, and all the while I had forgotten Tarn.

"I know not what high galleon shall come for thee, O King, nor what rowers, clad with purple, shall row at the bidding of gods when thou goest back with pomp to the river of Munra-O. But for me Tarn waits where the Seas of the West break over the edge of the world, and, as the years pass over me and the love of the chase sinks low, and as the glamour of the dark woods and mossy places dies down in my soul, ever louder and louder lap the ripples against the canoe of birch bark where, holding his twin-bladed oar, Tarn waits.

"But when my soul hath no more knowledge of the woods nor kindred any longer with the creatures of the dark, and when all that Tarn hath given it shall be lost, then Tarn shall take me back over the western seas, where all the remembered years lie floating idly a-swing with the ebb and flow, to bring me again to the river Munra-O. Far up that river we shall haply chase those creatures whose eyes are peering in the night as they prowl around the world, for Tarn was ever a hunter."

XI

Then Ulf spake, the prophet who in Sistrameides lives in a temple anciently dedicated to the gods. Rumour hath guessed that there the gods walked once some time towards evening. But Time whose hand is against the temples of the gods hath dealt harshly with it and overturned its pillars and set upon its ruins his sign and seal: now Ulf dwells there alone. And Ulf said, "There sets, O King, a river outward from earth which meets with a mighty sea whose waters roll through space and fling their billows on the shores of every star. These are the river and the sea of the Tears of Men."

And the King said:

"Men have not written of this sea."

And the prophet answered:

"Have not tears enough burst in the night time out of sleeping cities? Have not the sorrows of ten thousand homes sent streams into this river when twilight fell and it was still and there was none to hear? Have there not been hopes, and were they all fulfilled? Have there not been conquests and bitter defeats? And have not flowers when spring was over died in the gardens of many children? Tears enough, O King, tears enough have gone down out of earth to make such a sea; and deep it is and wide and the gods know it and it flings its spray on the shores of all the stars. Down this river and across this sea thou shalt fare in a ship of sighs and all around thee over the sea shall fly the prayers of men which rise on white wings higher than their sorrows. Sometimes perched in the rigging, sometimes crying around thee, shall go the prayers that availed not to stay thee in Zarkandhu. Far over the waters, and on the wings of the prayers beats the light of an inaccessible star. No hand hath touched it, none hath journeyed to it, it hath no substance, it is only a light, it is the star of Hope, and it shines far over the sea and brightens the world. It is nought but a light, but the gods gave it.

"Led only by the light of this star the myriad prayers that thou shalt see all around thee fly to the Hall of the gods.

"Sighs shall waft thy ship of sighs over the sea of Tears. Thou shalt pass by islands of laughter and lands of song lying low in the sea, and all of them drenched with tears flung over their rocks by the waves of the sea all driven by the sighs.

"But at last thou shalt come with the prayers of men to the great Hall of the gods where the chairs of the gods are carved of onyx grouped round the golden throne of the eldest of the gods. And there, O King, hope not to find the gods, but reclining upon the golden throne wearing a cloak of his master's thou shalt see the figure of Time with blood upon his hands, and loosely dangling from his fingers a dripping sword, and spattered with blood but empty shall stand the onyx chairs.

"There he sits on his master's throne dangling idly his sword, or with it flicking cruelly at the prayers of men that lie in a great heap bleeding at his feet.

"For a while, O King, the gods had sought to solve the riddles of Time, for a while They made him Their slave, and Time smiled and obeyed his masters, for a while, O King, for a while. He that hath spared nothing hath not spared the gods, nor yet shall he spare thee."

Then the King spake dolefully in the Hall of Kings, and said:

"May I not find at last the gods, and must it be that I may not look in Their faces at the last to see whether They be kindly? They that have sent me on my earthward journey I would greet on my returning, if not as a King coming again to his own city, yet as one who having been ordered had obeyed, and obeying had merited something of those for whom he toiled. I would look

Them in Their faces, O prophet, and ask Them concerning many things and would know the wherefore of much. I had hoped, O prophet, that those gods that had smiled upon my childhood, Whose voices stirred at evening in gardens when I was young, would hold dominion still when at last I came to seek Them. O prophet, if this is not to be, make you a great dirge for my childhood's gods and fashion silver bells and, setting them mostly a-swing amidst such trees as grew in the garden of my childhood, sing you this dirge in the dusk: and sing it when the low moth flies up and down and the bat first comes peering from her home; sing it when white mists come rising from the river, when smoke is pale and grey, while flowers are yet closing, ere voices are yet hushed; sing it while all things yet lament the day, or ever the great lights of heaven come blazing forth and night with her splendours takes the place of day. For, if the old gods die, let us lament Them or ever new knowledge comes, while all the world still shudders at Their loss.

"For at the last, O prophet, what is left? Only the gods of my childhood dead, and only Time striding large and lonely through the spaces, chilling the moon and paling the light of stars and scattering earthward out of both his hands the dust of forgetfulness over the fields of heroes and smitten Temples of the older gods."

But when the other prophets heard with what doleful words the King spake in the Hall they all cried out:

"It is not as Ulf has said but as I have said—and I."

Then the King pondered long, not speaking. But down in the city in a street between the houses stood grouped together they that were wont to dance before the King, and they that had borne his wine in jewelled cups. Long they had tarried in the city hoping that the King might relent, and once again regard them with kindly face calling for wine and song. The next morning they were all to set out in search of some new Kingdom, and they were peering between the houses and up the long grey street to see for the last time the palace of King Ebalon; and Pattering Leaves, the dancer, cried:

"Not any more, not any more at all shall we drift up the carven hall to dance before the King. He that now watches the magic of his prophets will behold no more the wonder of the dance, and among ancient parchments, strange and wise, he shall forget the swirl of drapery when we sing together through the Dance of the Myriad Steps."

And with her were Silvern Fountain and Summer Lightning and Dream of the Sea, each lamenting that they should dance no more to please the eyes of the King.

And Intahn who had carried at the banquet for fifty years the goblet of the King set with its four sapphires each as large as an eye, said as he spread his hands towards the palace making the sign of farewell:

"Not all the magic of prophecy nor yet foreseeing nor preceiving may equal the power of wine. Through the small door in the King's Hall one goes by one hundred steps and many sloping corridors into the cool of the earth where lies a cavern vaster than the Hall. Therein, curtained by the spider, repose the casks of wine that are wont to gladden the hearts of the Kings of Zarkandhu. In islands far to the eastward the vine, from whose heart this wine was long since wrung, hath climbed aloft with many a clutching finger and beheld the sea and ships of the olden time and men since dead, and gone down into the earth again and been covered over with weeds. And green with the damp of the years there lie three casks that a city gave not up until all her defenders were slain and her houses fired; and ever to the soul of that wine is added a more ardent fire as ever the years go by. Thither it was my pride to go before the banquet in the olden years and coming up to bear in the sapphire goblet the fire of the elder Kings and to watch the King's eye flash and his face grow nobler and more like his sires as he drank the gleaming wine.

"And now the King seeks wisdom from his prophets while all the glory of the past and all the clattering splendour of to-day grows old, far down, forgotten beneath his feet."

And when he ceased the cupbearers and the women that danced looked long in silence at the palace. Then one by one all made the farewell sign before they turned to go, and as they did this a herald unseen in the dark was speeding towards them.

After a long silence the King spake:

"Prophets of my Kingdom," he said, "you have not prophesied alike, and the words of each prophet condemn his fellows' words so that wisdom may not be discovered among prophets. But I command that none in my Kingdom shall doubt that the earliest King of Zarkandhu stored wine beneath this palace before the building of the city or ever the palace arose, and I shall cause commands to be uttered for the making of a banquet at once within this Hall, so that ye shall perceive that the power of my wine is greater than all your spells, and dancing more wondrous that prophecy."

The dancers and the winebearers were summoned back, and as the night wore on a banquet was spread and all the prophets bidden to be seated, Samahn, Ynath, Monith, Ynar Thun, the prophet of Journeys, Zornadhu, Yamen, Paharn, Ilana, Ulf, and one that had not spoken nor yet revealed his name, and who wore his prophet's cloak across his face.

And the prophets feasted as they were commanded and spake as other men spake, save he whose face was hidden, who neither ate nor spake. Once he put out his hand from under his cloak and touched a blossom among the flowers upon the table and the blossom fell.

And Pattering Leaves came in and danced again, and the King smiled, and Pattering Leaves was happy though she had not the wisdom of the prophets. And in and out, in and out, in and out among the columns of the Hall went Summer Lightning in the maze of the dance. And Silvern Fountain bowed before the King and danced and danced and bowed again, and old Intahn went to and fro from the cavern to the King gravely through the midst of the dancers but with kindly eyes, and when the King had often drunk of the old wine of

the elder Kings he called for Dream of the Sea and bade
her sing. And Dream of the Sea came through the arches
and sang of an island builded by magic out of pearls,
that lay set in a ruby sea, and how it lay far off and
under the south, guarded by jagged reefs whereon the
sorrows of the world were wrecked and never came to
the island. And how a low sunset always reddened the
sea and lit the magic isle and never turned to night, and
how someone sang always and endlessly to lure the
soul of a King who might by enchantment pass the
guarding reefs to find rest on the pearl island and not
be troubled more, but only see sorrows on the outer
reef battered and broken. Then Soul of the South rose
up and sang a song of a fountain that ever sought to
reach the sky and was ever doomed to fall to the earth
again until at last . . .

Then whether it was the art of Pattering Leaves or
the song of Dream of the Sea, or whether it was the
fire of the wine of the elder Kings, Ebalon bade farewell
kindly to the prophets when morning paled the stars.
Then along the torchlit corridors the King went to his
chamber, and having shut the door in the empty room,
beheld suddenly a figure wearing the cloak of a prophet;
and the King perceived that it was he whose face was
hidden at the banquet, who had not revealed his name.

And the King said:

"Art thou, too, a prophet?"

And the figure answered:

"I am a prophet."

And the King said: "Knowest *thou* aught concerning
the journey of the King?" And the figure answered: "I
know, but have never said."

And the King said: "Who art thou that knowest so
much and hast not told it?"

And he answered:

"I am THE END."

Then the cloaked figure strode away from the palace;
and the King, unseen by the guards, followed upon his
journey.

The Fall of Babbulkund

I said: "I will arise now and see Babbulkund, City of Marvel. She is of one age with the earth; the stars are her sisters. Pharaohs of the old time coming conquering from Araby first saw her, a solitary mountain in the desert, and cut the mountain into towers and terraces. They destroyed one of the hills of God, but they made Babbulkund. She is carven, not built; her palaces are one with her terraces, there is neither join nor cleft. Hers is the beauty of the youth of the world. She deemeth herself to be the middle of Earth, and hath four gates facing outward to the Nations. There sits outside her eastern gate a colossal god of stone. His face flushes with the lights of dawn. When the morning sunlight warms his lips they part a little, and he giveth utterance to the words 'Oon Oom,' and the language is long since dead in which he speaks, and all his worshippers are gathered to their tombs, so that none knoweth what the words portend that he uttereth at dawn. Some say that he greets the sun as one god greets another in the language thereof, and others say that he proclaims the day, and others that he uttereth warning. And at every gate is a marvel not credible until beholden."

And I gathered three friends and said to them: "We are what we have seen and known. Let us journey now and behold Babbulkund, that our minds may be beautified with it and our spirits made holier."

So we took ship and travelled over the lifting sea, and remembered not things done in the towns we knew, but laid away the thoughts of them like soiled linen and put them by, and dreamed of Babbulkund.

But when we came to the land of which Babbulkund

is the abiding glory, we hired a caravan of camels and Arab guides, and passed southwards in the afternoon on the three days' journey through the desert that should bring us to the white walls of Babbulkund. And the heat of the sun shone upon us out of the bright grey sky, and the heat of the desert beat up at us from below.

About sunset we halted and tethered our horses, while the Arabs unloaded the provisions from the camels and prepared a fire out of the dry scrub, for at sunset the heat of the desert departs from it suddenly, like a bird. Then we saw a traveller approaching us on a camel coming from the south. When he was come near we said to him:

"Come and encamp among us, for in the desert all men are brothers, and we will give thee meat to eat and wine, or, if thou art bound by thy faith, we will give thee some other drink that is not accursed by the prophet."

The traveller seated himself beside us on the sand, and crossed his legs and answered:

"Hearken, and I will tell you of Babbulkund, City of Marvel. Babbulkund stands just below the meeting of the rivers, where Oonrāna, River of Myth, flows into the Waters of Fable, even the old stream Plegathanees. These, together, enter her northern gate rejoicing. Of old they flowed in the dark through the Hill that Nehemoth, the first of Pharaohs, carved into the City of Marvel. Sterile and desolate they float far through the desert, each in the appointed cleft, with life upon neither bank, but give birth in Babbulkund to the sacred purple garden whereof all nations sing. Thither all the bees come on a pilgrimage at evening by a secret way of the air. Once, from his twilit kingdom, which he rules equally with the sun, the moon saw and loved Babbulkund, clad with her purple garden; and the moon wooed Babbulkund, and she sent him weeping away, for she is more beautiful than all her sisters the stars. Her sisters come to her at night into her maiden chamber. Even the gods speak sometimes of Babbulkund, clad with her purple garden. Listen, for I perceive by your eyes that ye have not seen Babbulkund; there is a restlessness in them and an unappeased wonder. Listen. In the garden whereof I spoke there is a lake that hath no twin or fellow in the world; there is no companion for it among all the lakes. The shores of it are of glass, and the bottom of it. In it are great fish having golden and scarlet scales, and they swim to and fro. Here it is the wont of the eighty-second Nehemoth (who rules in the city to-day) to come, after the dusk has fallen, and sit by the lake alone, and at this hour eight hundred slaves go down by steps through caverns into vaults beneath the lake. Four hundred of them carrying purple lights march one behind the other, from east to west, and four hundred carrying green lights march one behind the other, from west to east. The two lines cross and re-cross each other in and out as the slaves go round and round, and the fearful fish flash up and down and to and fro."

But upon that traveller speaking night descended, solemn and cold, and we wrapped ourselves in our blankets and lay down upon the sand in the sight of the astral sisters of Babbulkund. And all that night the desert said many things, softly and in a whisper, but I knew not what he said. Only the sand knew and arose and was troubled and lay down again, and the wind knew. Then, as the hours of the night went by, these two discovered the foot-tracks wherewith we had disturbed the holy desert, and they troubled over them and covered them up; and then the wind lay down and the sand rested. Then the wind arose again and the sand danced. This they did many times. And all the while the desert whispered what I shall not know.

Then I slept awhile and awoke just before sunrise, very cold. Suddenly the sun leapt up and flamed upon our faces; we all threw off our blankets and stood up. Then we took food, and afterwards started southwards, and in the heat of the day rested, and afterwards pushed on again. And all the while the desert remained the same, like a dream that will not cease to trouble a tired sleeper.

And often travellers passed us in the desert, coming from the City of Marvel, and there was a light and a glory in their eyes from having seen Babbulkund.

That evening, at sunset, another traveller neared us, and we hailed him, saying:

"Wilt thou eat and drink with us, seeing that all men are brothers in the desert?"

And he descended from his camel and sat by us and said:

"When morning shines on the colossus Neb and Neb speaks, at once the musicians of King Nehemoth in Babbulkund awake.

"At first their fingers wander over their golden harps, or they stroke idly their violins. Clearer and clearer the note of each instrument ascends like larks arising from the dew, till suddenly they all blend together and a new melody is born. Thus, every morning, the musicians of King Nehemoth make a new marvel in the City of Marvel; for these are no common musicians, but masters of melody, raided by conquest long since, and carried away in ships from the Isles of Song. And, at the sound of the music, Nehemoth awakes in the eastern chamber of his palace, which is carved in the form of a great crescent, four miles long, on the northern side of the city. Full in the windows of its eastern chamber the sun rises, and full in the windows of its western chamber the sun sets.

"When Nehemoth awakes he summons slaves who bring a palanquin with bells, which the King enters, having lightly robed. Then the slaves run and bear him to the onyx Chamber of the Bath, with the sound of small bells ringing as they run. And when Nehemoth emerges thence, bathed and anointed, the slaves run on with their ringing palanquin and bear him to the Orient Chamber of Banquets, where the King takes the first meal of the day. Thence, through the great white corridor whose windows all face sunwards, Nehemoth, in his planquin, passes on to the Audience Chamber of Embassies from the North, which is all decked with Northern wares.

"All about it are ornaments of amber from the North and carven chalices of the dark brown Northern crystal, and on its floors lie furs from Baltic shores.

"In adjoining chambers are stored the wonted food of the hardy Northern men, and the strong wine of the North, pale but terrible. Therein the King receives barbarian princes from the frigid lands. Thence the slaves bear him swiftly to the Audience Chamber of Embassies from the East, where the walls are of turquoise, studded with the rubies of Ceylon, where the gods are the gods of the East, where all the hangings have been devised in the gorgeous heart of Ind, and where all the carvings have been wrought with the cunning of the isles. Here, if a caravan hath chanced to have come in from Ind or from Cathay, it is the King's wont to converse awhile with Moguls or Mandarins, for from the East come the arts and knowledge of the world, and the converse of their people is polite. Thus Nehemoth passes on through the other Audience Chambers and receives, perhaps, some Sheikhs of the Arab folk who have crossed the great desert from the West, or receives an embassy sent to do him homage from the shy jungle people to the South. And all the while the slaves with the ringing palanquin run westwards, following the sun, and ever the sun shines straight into the chamber where Nehemoth sits, and all the while the music from one or other of his bands of musicians comes tinkling to his ears. But when the middle of the day draws near, the slaves run to the cool groves that lie along the verandahs on the northern side of the palace, forsaking the sun, and as the heat overcomes the genius of the musicians, one by one their hands fall from their instruments, till at last all melody ceases. At this moment Nehemoth falls asleep, and the slaves put the palanquin down and lie down beside it. At this hour the city becomes quite still, and the palace of Nehemoth and the tombs of the Pharaohs of old face to the sunlight, all alike in silence. Even the jewellers in the market-place, selling gems to princes, cease from their bargaining and cease to sing; for in Babbulkund the vendor of rubies sings the song of the ruby, and the vendor of sapphires sings the song of the sapphire, and each stone hath its song, so that a man, by his song, proclaims and makes known his wares.

"But all these sounds cease at the meridian hour, the jewellers in the market-place lie down in what shadow they can find, and the princes go back to the cool places in their palaces, and a great hush in the gleaming air hangs over Babbulkund. But in the cool of the late afternoon, one of the King's musicians will awake from dreaming of his home and will pass his fingers, perhaps, over the strings of his harp and, with the music, some memory may arise of the wind in the glens of the mountains that stand in the Isles of Song. Then the musician will wrench great cries out of the soul of his harp for the sake of the old memory, and his fellows will awake and all make a song of home, woven of sayings told in the harbour when the ships came in, and of tales in the cottages about the people of old time. One by one the other bands of musicians will take up the song, and Babbulkund, City of Marvel, will throb with this marvel anew. Just now Nehemoth awakes, the slaves leap to their feet and bear the palanquin to the outer side of the great crescent palace between the south and the west, to behold the sun again. The palanquin, with its ringing bells, goes round once more; the voices of the jewellers sing again, in the market-place, the song of the emerald, the song of the sapphire; men talk on the housetops, beggars wail in the streets, the musicians bend to their work, all the sound blend together into one murmur, the voice of Babbulkund speaking at evening. Lower and lower sinks the sun, till Nehemoth, following it, comes with his panting slaves to the great purple garden of which

surely thine own country has its song, from wherever
thou art come.

"There he alights from his palanquin and goes up
to a throne of ivory set in the garden's midst, facing full
westwards, and sits there alone, long regarding the
sunlight until it is quite gone. At this hour trouble
comes into the face of Nehemoth. Men have heard him
muttering at the time of sunset: 'Even I too, even I too.'
Thus do King Nehemoth and the sun make their glorious ambits about Babbulkund.

"A little later, when the stars come out to envy the
beauty of the City of Marvel, the King walks to another
part of the garden and sits in an alcove of opal all
alone by the marge of the sacred lake. This is the lake
whose shores and floors are of glass, which is lit from
beneath by slaves with purple lights and with green
lights intermingling, and is one of the seven wonders
of Babbulkund. Three of the wonders are in the city's
midst and four are at her gates. There is the lake, of
which I tell thee, and the purple garden of which I
have told thee and which is a wonder even to the stars,
and there is Ong Zwarba, of which I shall tell thee also.
And the wonders at the gates are these. At the eastern
gate Neb. And at the northern gate the wonder of the
river and the arches, for the River of Myth, which becomes one with the Waters of Fable in the desert outside the city, floats under a gate of pure gold, rejoicing,
and under many arches fantastically carven that are one
with either bank. The marvel at the western gate is the
marvel of Annolith and the dog Voth. Annolith sits outside the western gate facing towards the city. He is higher than any of the towers or palaces, for his head was
carved from the summit of the old hill; he hath two
eyes of sapphire wherewith he regards Babbulkund, and
the wonder of the eyes is that they are to-day in the
same sockets wherein they glowed when first the world
began, only the marble that covered them has been
carven away and the light of day let in and the sight
of the envious stars. Larger than a lion is the dog Voth

beside him; every hair is carven upon the back of Voth, his war hackles are erected and his teeth are bared. All the Nehemoths have worshipped the gold Annolith, but all their people pray to the dog Voth, for the law of the land is that none but a Nehemoth may worship the god Annolith. The marvel at the southern gate is the marvel of the jungle, for he comes with all his wild untravelled sea of darkness and trees and tigers and sunward-aspiring orchids right through a marble gate in the city wall and enters the city, and there widens and holds a space in its midst of many miles across. Moreover, he is older than the city of Marvel, for he dwelt long since in one of the valleys of the mountain which Nehemoth, first of Pharaohs, carved into Babbulkund.

"Now the opal alcove in which the King sits at evening by the lake stands at the edge of the jungle, and the climbing orchids of the jungle have long since crept from their homes through clefts of the opal alcove, lured by the lights of the lake, and now bloom there exultingly. Near to this alcove are the hareems of Nehemoth.

"The King hath four hareems—one for the stalwart women from the mountains to the north, one for the dark and furtive jungle women, one for the desert women that have wandering souls and pine in Babbulkund, and one for the princesses of his own kith, whose brown cheeks blush with the blood of ancient Pharaohs and who exult with Babbulkund in her surpassing beauty, and who know nought of the desert or the jungle or the bleak hills to the north. Quite unadorned and clad in simple garments go all the kith of Nehemoth, for they know well that he grows weary of pomp. Unadorned all save one, the Princess Linderith, who weareth Ong Zwarba and the three lesser gems of the sea. Such a stone is Ong Zwarba that there are none like it even in the turban of Nehemoth nor in all the sanctuaries of the sea. The same god that made Linderith made long ago Ong Zwarba; she and Ong Zwarba shine together with one light, and beside this marvellous stone gleam the three lesser ones of the sea.

"Now when the King sitteth in his opal alcove by the sacred lake with the orchids blooming around him all sounds are become still. The sound of the tramping of the weary slaves as they go round and round never comes to the surface. Long since the musicians sleep, and their hands have fallen dumb upon their instruments, and the voices in the city have died away. Perhaps a sigh of one of the desert women has become half a song, or on a hot night in summer one of the women of the hills sings softly a song of snow; all night long in the midst of the purple garden sings one nightingale; all else is still; the stars that look on Babbulkund arise and set, the cold unhappy moon drifts lonely through them, the night wears on; at last the dark figure of Nehemoth, eighty-second of his line, rises and moves stealthily away."

The traveller ceased to speak. For a long time the clear stars, sisters of Babbulkund, had shone upon him speaking, the desert wind had arisen and whispered to the sand, and the sand had long gone secretly to and fro; none of us had moved, none of us had fallen asleep, not so much from wonder at his tale as from the thought that we ourselves in two days' time should see that wondrous city. Then we wrapped our blankets around us and lay down with our feet towards the embers of our fire and instantly were asleep, and in our dreams we multiplied the fame of the City of Marvel.

The sun arose and flamed upon our faces, and all the desert glinted with its light. Then we stood up and prepared the morning meal, and, when we had eaten, the traveller departed. And we commended his soul to the god of the land whereto he went, of the land of his home to the northward, and he commended our souls to the God of the people of the land wherefrom we had come. Then a traveller overtook us going on foot; he wore a brown cloak that was all in rags and he seemed to have been walking all night, and he walked hurriedly but appeared weary, so we offered him food and drink, of which he partook thankfully. When we asked him where he was going, he answered "Babbulkund." Then we offered him a camel upon which to ride, for we said, "We also go to Babbulkund." But he answered strangely:

"Nay, pass on before me, for it is a sore thing never to have seen Babbulkund, having lived while yet she stood. Pass on before me and behold her, and then flee away at once, returning northward."

Then, though we understood him not, we left him, for he was insistent, and passed on our journey southwards through the desert, and we came before the middle of the day to an oasis of palm trees standing by a well and there we gave water to the haughty camels and replenished our water-bottles and soothed our eyes with the sight of green things and tarried for many hours in the shade. Some of the men slept, but of those that remained awake each man sang softly the songs of his own country, telling of Babbulkund. When the afternoon was far spent we travelled a little way southwards, and went on through the cool evening until the sun fell low and we encamped, and as we sat in our encampment the man in rags overtook us, having travelled all the day, and we gave him food and drink again, and in the twilight he spoke, saying:

"I am the servant of the Lord the God of my people, and I go to do his work on Babbulkund. She is the most beautiful city in the world; there hath been none like her, even the stars of God go envious of her beauty. She is all white, yet with streaks of pink that pass through her streets and houses like flames in the white mind of a sculptor, like desire in Paradise. She hath been carved of old out of a holy hill, no slaves wrought the City of Marvel, but artists toiling at the work they loved. They took no pattern from the houses of men, but each man wrought what his inner eye had seen and carved in marble the visions of his dream. All over the roof of one of the palace chambers winged lions flit like bats, the size of every one is the size of the lions of God, and the wings are larger than any wing created; they are one above the other more than a man can number, they are all carven out of one block of marble, the chamber itself is hollowed from it, and it is borne aloft upon the carven branches of a grove of clustered tree-ferns wrought by the hand of some jungle mason that loved the tall fern well. Over the River of Myth, which is one with the Waters of Fable, go bridges, fashioned like the wisteria tree and like the drooping laburnum, and a hundred others of wonderful devices, the desire of the souls of masons a long while dead. Oh! very beautiful is white Babbulkund, very beautiful she is, but proud; and the Lord the God of my people hath seen her in her pride, and looking towards her hath seen the prayers of Nehemoth going up to the abomination Annolith, and all the people following after Voth. She is very beautiful, Babbulkund; alas, that I may not bless her. I could live always on one of her inner terraces looking on the mysterious jungle in her midst and the heavenward faces of the orchids that, clambering from the darkness, behold the sun. I could love Babbulkund with a great love, yet am I the servant of the Lord the God of my people, and the King hath sinned unto the abomination Annolith, and the people lust exceedingly for Voth. Alas for thee, Babbulkund, alas that I may not even now turn back, for to-morrow I must prophesy against thee and cry out against thee, Babbulkund. But ye travellers that have entreated me hospitably, rise and pass on with your camels, for I can tarry no longer, and I go to do the work on Babbulkund of the Lord the God of my people. Go now and see the beauty of Babbulkund before I cry out against her, and then flee swiftly northwards."

A smouldering fragment fell in upon our camp fire and sent a strange light into the eyes of the man in rags. He rose at once, and his tattered cloak swirled up with him like a great wing; he said no more, but turned

round from us instantly southwards, and strode away
into the darkness towards Babbulkund. Then a hush fell
upon our encampment, and the smell of the tobacco
of those lands arose. When the last flame died down in
our camp fire I fell asleep, but my rest was troubled by
shifting dreams of doom.

Morning came, and our guides told us that we should
come to the city ere nightfall. Again we passed southwards through the changeless desert; sometimes we met
travellers coming from Babbulkund, with the beauty of
its marvels still fresh in their eyes.

When we encamped near the middle of the day we
saw a great number of people on foot coming towards
us running, from the southwards. These we hailed when
they were come near, saying, "What of Babbulkund?"

They answered: "We are not of the race of the people
of Babbulkund, but were captured in youth and taken
away from the hills that are to the northward. Now we
have all seen in visions of the stillness the Lord the God
of our people calling to us from His hills, and therefore
we all flee northward. But in Babbulkund King Nehemoth hath been troubled in the nights by unkingly
dreams of doom, and none may interpret what the
dreams portend. Now this is the dream that King
Nehemoth dreamed on the first night of his dreaming.
He saw move through the stillness a bird all black,
and beneath the beatings of his wings Babbulkund
gloomed and darkened; and after him flew a bird all
white, beneath the beatings of whose wings Babbulkund
gleamed and shone; and there flew by four more birds
alternately black and white. And, as the black ones
passed Babbulkund darkened, and when the white ones
appeared her streets and houses shone. But after the
sixth bird there came no more, and Babbulkund vanished from her place, and there was only the empty
desert where she had stood, and the rivers Oonrāna and
Plegathanees mourning alone. Next morning all the
prophets of the King gathered before their abominations and questioned them of the dream, and the abomi-

nations spake not. But when the second night stepped
down from the halls of God, dowered with many stars,
King Nehemoth dreamed again; and in this dream
King Nehemoth saw four birds only, black and white
alternately as before. And Babbulkund darkened again
as the black ones passed, and shone when the white
came by; only after the four birds came no more, and
Babbulkund vanished from her place, leaving only the
forgetful desert and the mourning rivers.

"Still the abominations spake not, and none could
interpret the dream. And when the third night came
forth from the divine halls of her home dowered like
her sisters, again King Nehemoth dreamed. And he
saw a bird all black go by again, beneath whom Babbulkund darkened, and then a white bird and Babbulkund
shone; and after them came no more, and Babbulkund
passed away. And the golden day appeared, dispelling
dreams, and still the abominations were silent, and the
King's prophets answered not to portend the omen of
the dream. One prophet only spake before the King,
saying: 'The sable birds, O King, are the nights, and
the white birds are the days. . . .' This thing the King
had feared, and he arose and smote the prophet with
his sword, whose soul went crying away and had to do
no more with nights and days.

"It was last night that the King dreamed his third
dream, and this morning we fled away from Babbulkund. A great heat lies over it, and the orchids of the
jungle droop their heads. All night long the women in
the hareem of the North have wailed horribly for their
hills. A fear hath fallen upon the city, and a boding.
Twice hath Nehemoth gone to worship Annolith, and
all the people have prostrated themselves before Voth.
Thrice the horologers have looked into the great crystal
globe wherein are foretold all happenings to be, and
thrice the globe was blank. Yea, though they went a
fourth time yet was no vision revealed; and the people's
voice is hushed in Babbulkund."

Soon the travellers arose and pushed on northwards

again, leaving us wondering. Through the heat of the day we rested as well as we might, but the air was motionless and sultry and the camels ill at ease. The Arabs said that it boded a desert storm, and that a great wind would arise full of sand. So we arose in the afternoon, and travelled swiftly, hoping to come to shelter before the storm. And the air burned in the stillness between the baked desert and the glaring sky.

Suddenly a wind arose out of the South, blowing from Babbulkund, and the sand lifted and went by in great shapes, all whispering. And the wind blew violently, and wailed as it blew, and hundreds of sandy shapes went towering by, and there were little cries among them and the sounds of a passing away. Soon the wind sank quite suddenly, and its cries died, and the panic ceased among the driven sands. And when the storm departed the air was cool, and the terrible sultriness and the boding were passed away, and the camels had ease among them. And the Arabs said that the storm which was to be had been, as was willed of old by God.

The sun set and the gloaming came, and we neared the junction of Oonrāna and Plegathanees, but in the darkness discerned not Babbulkund. We pushed on hurriedly to reach the city ere nightfall, and came to the junction of the River of Myth where he meets with the Waters of Fable, and still saw not Babbulkund. All round us lay the sand and rocks of the unchanging desert, save to the southwards were the jungle stood with its orchids facing skywards. Then we perceived that we had arrived too late, and that her doom had come to Babbulkund; and by the river in the empty desert on the sand the man in rags was seated, with his face hidden in his hands, weeping bitterly.

Thus passed away in the hour of her iniquities before Annolith, in the two thousand and thirty-second year of her being, in the six thousand and fiftieth year of the building of the World, Babbulkund, City of Marvel, sometime called by those that hated her City of the Dog, but hourly mourned in Araby and Ind and wide through jungle and desert; leaving no memorial in stone to show that she had been, but remembered with an abiding love, in spite of the anger of God, by all that knew her beauty, whereof still they sing.

The Bird of the Difficult Eye

Observant men and women that know their Bond Street well will appreciate my astonishment when in a jewellers' shop I perceived that nobody was furtively watching me. Not only this but when I even picked up a little carved crystal to examine it no shop-assistants crowded round me. I walked the whole length of the shop, still no one politely followed.

Seeing from this that some extraordinary revolution had occurred in the jewelry business I went with my curiosity well aroused to a queer old person half demon and half man who has an idol-shop in a byway of the City and who keeps me informed of affairs of the Edge of the World. And briefly over a pinch of heather incense that he takes by way of snuff he gave me this tremendous information: that Mr. Neepy Thang, the son of Thangobrind, had returned from the Edge of the World and was even now in London.

The information may not appear tremendous to those unacquainted with the source of jewelry; but when I say that the only thief employed by any West-end jeweller since famous Thangobrind's distressing doom is this same Neepy Thang, and that for lightness of fingers and swiftness of stockinged foot they have none better in Paris, it will be understood why the Bond-street jewellers no longer cared what became of their old stock.

There were big diamonds in London that summer and a few considerable sapphires. In certain astounding kingdoms behind the East strange sovereigns missed from their turbans the heirlooms of ancient wars, and here and there the keepers of crown jewels who had not heard the stockinged feet of Thang, were questioned and died slowly.

And the jewellers gave a little dinner to Thang at the Hotel Great Magnificent; the windows had not been opened for five years and there was wine at a guinea a bottle that you could not tell from champagne and cigars at half a crown with a Havana label. Altogether it was a splendid evening for Thang.

But I have to tell of a far sadder thing than a dinner at a hotel. The public require jewelry and jewelry must be obtained. I have to tell of Neepy Thang's last journey.

That year the fashion was emeralds. A man named Green had recently crossed the Channel on a bicycle and the jewellers said that a green stone would be particularly appropriate to commemorate the event and recommended emeralds.

Now a certain money-lender of Cheapside who had just been made a peer had divided his gains into three equal parts; one for the purchase of the peerage, country-house and park, and the twenty thousand pheasants that are absolutely essential, and one for the upkeep of the position, while the third he banked abroad, partly to cheat the native tax-gatherer and partly because it seemed to him that the days of the Peerage were few and that he might at any moment be called upon to start afresh elsewhere. In the upkeep of the position he included jewellry for his wife and so it came about that Lord Castlenorman placed an order with two well-known Bond-street jewellers named Messrs. Grosvenor and Campbell to the extent of £100,000 for a few reliable emeralds.

But the emeralds in stock were mostly small and shop-soiled and Neepy Thang had to set out at once before he had had as much as a week in London. I will briefly sketch his project. Not many knew it, for where the form of business is blackmail the fewer creditors you have the better (which of course in various degrees applies at all times).

On the shores of the risky seas of Shiroora Shan grows one tree only so that upon its branches if anywhere in the world there must build its nest the Bird of the Difficult Eye. Neepy Thang had come by this information, which was indeed the truth, that if the bird migrated to Fairyland before the three eggs hatched out they would undoubtedly all turn into emeralds, while if they hatched out first it would be a bad business.

When he had mentioned these eggs to Messrs. Grosvenor and Campbell they had said, "The very thing": they were men of few words, in English, for it was not their native tongue.

So Neepy Thang set out. He bought the purple ticket at Victoria Station. He went by Herne Hill, Bromley and Bickley and passed St. Mary Cray. At Eynsford he changed and taking a footpath along a winding valley went wandering into the hills. And at the top of a hill in a little wood, where all the anemones long since were over and the perfume of mint and thyme from outside came drifting in with Thang, he found once more the familiar path, age-old and fair as wonder, that leads to the Edge of the World. Little to him were its sacred memories that are one with the secret of earth, for he was out on business, and little would they be to me if I ever put them on paper. Let it suffice that he went down that path going further and further from the fields we know, and all the way he muttered to himself, "What if the eggs hatch out and it be a bad business!" The glamour that is at all times upon those lonely lands that lie at the back of the chalky hills of Kent intensified as he went upon his journeys. Queerer and queerer grew the things that he saw by little World-End Path. Many a twilight dscended upon that journey with all their mysteries, many a blaze of stars; many a morning came flaming up to a tinkle of silvern horns; till the outpost elves of Fairyland came in sight and the glittering crests of Fairyland's three mountains betokened the journey's end. And so with painful steps (for the shores of the world are covered with huge crystals) he came to the risky seas of Shiroora Shan and saw them pounding to gravel the wreckage of fallen stars, saw them and heard their roar, those shipless seas that between earth and the fairies' homes heave beneath some huge wind that is none of our four. And there in the darkness on the grizzly coast, for darkness was swooping slantwise down the sky as though with some evil purpose, there stood that lonely, gnarled and deciduous tree. It was a bad place to be found in after dark, and night descended with multitudes of stars, beasts prowling in the blackness gluttered* at Neepy Thang. And there on a lower branch within easy reach he clearly saw the Bird of the Difficult Eye sitting upon the nest for which she is famous. Her face was towards those three inscrutable mountains, far-off on the other side of the risky seas, whose hidden valleys are Fairyland. Though not yet autumn in the fields we know, it was close on midwinter here, the moment as Thang knew well when those eggs hatch out. Had he miscalculated and arrived a minute too late? Yet the bird was even now about to migrate, her pinions fluttered and her gaze was toward Fairyland. Thang hoped and muttered a prayer to those pagan gods whose spite and vengeance he had most reason to fear. It seems that it was too late or a prayer too small to placate them, for there and then the stroke of mid-winter came and the eggs hatched out in the roar of Shiroora Shan or ever the bird was gone with her difficult eye and it was a bad business indeed for Neepy Thang; I haven't the heart to tell you any more.

" 'Ere," said Lord Castlenorman some few weeks later to Messrs. Grosvenor and Campbell, "you aren't 'arf taking your time about those emeralds."

*See any dictionary, but in vain.

The Secret of the Sea

In an ill-lit ancient tavern that I know, are many tales of the sea; but not without the wine of Gorgondy, that I had of a private bargain from the gnomes, was the tale laid bare for which I had waited of an evening for the greater part of a year.

I knew my man and listened to his stories, sitting amid the bluster of his oaths; I plied him with rum and whiskey and mixed drinks, but there never came the tale for which I sought, and as a last resort I went to the Huthneth Mountains and bargained there all night with the chiefs of the gnomes.

When I came to the ancient tavern and entered the low-roofed room, bringing the hoard of the gnomes in a bottle of hammered iron, my man had not yet arrived. The sailors laughed at my old iron bottle, but I sat down and waited; had I opened it then they would have wept and sung. I was well content to wait, for I knew my man had the story, and it was such a one as had profoundly stirred the incredulity of the faithless.

He entered and greeted me, and sat down and called for brandy. He was a hard man to turn from his purpose, and, uncorking my iron bottle, I sought to dissuade him from brandy for fear that when the brandy bit his throat he should refuse to leave it for any other wine. He lifted his head and said deep and dreadful things of any man that should dare to speak against brandy.

I swore that I said nothing against brandy but added that it was often given to children, while Gorgondy was only drunk by men of such depravity that they had abandoned sin because all the usual vices had come to seem genteel. When he asked if Gorgondy was a bad wine to drink I said that it was so bad that if a man sipped it that was the one touch that made damnation certain. Then he asked me what I had in the iron bottle, and I said it was Gorgondy; and then he shouted for the largest tumbler in that ill-lit ancient tavern, and stood up and shook his fist at me when it came, and swore, and told me to fill it with the wine that I got on that bitter night from the treasure house of the gnomes.

As he drank it he told me that he had met men who had spoken against wine, and that they had mentioned Heaven; and therefore he would not go there—no, not he; and that once he had sent one of them to Hell, but when he got there he would turn him out, and he had no use for milksops.

Over the second tumbler he was thoughtful, but still he said no word of the tale he knew, until I feared that it would never be heard. But when the third glass of that terrific wine had burned its way down his gullet, and vindicated the wickedness of the gnomes, his reticence withered like a leaf in the fire, and he bellowed out the secret.

I had long known that there is in ships a will or way of their own, and had even suspected that when sailors die or abandon their ships at sea, a derelict, being left to her own devices, may seek her own ends; but I had never dreamed by night, or fancied during the day, that the ships had a god that they worshipped, or that they secretly slipped away to a temple in the sea.

Over the fourth glass of the wine that the gnomes so sinfully brew but have kept so wisely from man, until the bargain that I had with their elders all through that autumn night, the sailor told me the story. I do not tell it as he told it to me because of the oaths that were in it; nor is it from delicacy that I refrain from writing these oaths verbatim, but merely because the horror they caused in me at the time troubles me still whenever I put them on paper, and I continue to shudder until I have blotted them out. Therefore, I tell the story in my own words, which, if they possess a certain decency that was not in the mouth of that sailor, unfortunately do not smack, as he did, of rum and blood and the sea.

You would take a ship to be a dead thing like a table, as dead as bits of iron and canvas and wood. That is because you always live on shore, and have never seen the sea, and drink milk. Milk is a more accursed drink than water.

What with the captain and what with the man at the wheel, and what with the crew, a ship has no fair chance of showing a will of her own.

There is only one moment in the history of ships, that carry crews on board, when they act by their own free will. This moment comes when all the crew are drunk. As the last man falls drunk on to the deck, the ship is free of man, and immediately slips away. She slips away at once on a new course and is never one yard out in a hundred miles.

It was like this one night with the Sea-Fancy. Bill Smiles was there himself, and can vouch for it. Bill Smiles has never told this tale before for fear that anyone should call him a liar. Nobody dislikes being hung as much as Bill Smiles would, but he won't be called a liar. I tell the tale as I heard it, relevancies and irrelevancies, though in my more decent words; and as I made no doubts of the truth of it then, I hardly like to now; others can please themselves.

It is not often that the whole of a crew is drunk. The crew of the Sea-Fancy was no drunkener than others. It happened like this.

The captain was always drunk. One day a fancy he had that some spiders were plotting against him, or a sudden bleeding he had from both his ears, made him think that drinking might be bad for his health. Next day he signed the pledge. He was sober all that morning and all the afternoon, but at evening he saw a sailor drinking a glass of beer, and a fit of madness seized him, and he said things that seemed bad to Bill Smiles. And next morning he made all of them take the pledge.

For two days nobody had a drop to drink, unless you count water, and on the third morning the captain was quite drunk. It stood to reason they all had a glass or two then, except the man at the wheel; and towards evening the man at the wheel could bear it no longer, and seems to have had his glass like all the rest, for the ship's course wobbled a bit and made a circle or two. Then all of a sudden she went off south by east under full canvas till midnight, and never altered her course. And at midnight she came to the wide wet courts of the Temple in the Sea.

People who think that Mr. Smiles is drunk often make a great mistake. And people are not the only ones that have made that mistake. Once a ship made it, and a lot of ships. It's a mistake to think that old Bill Smiles is drunk just because he can't move.

Midnight and moonlight and the Temple in the Sea Bill Smiles clearly remembers, and all the derelicts in the world were there, the old abandoned ships. The figureheads were nodding to themselves and blinking at the image. The image was a woman of white marble on a pedestal in the outer court of the Temple of the Sea: she was clearly the love of all the man-deserted ships, or the goddess to whom they prayed their heathen prayers. And as Bill Smiles was watching them, the lips of the figureheads moved; they all began to pray. But all at once their lips were closed with a snap when they saw that there were men on the Sea-Fancy. They all came crowding up and nodded and nodded and nodded to see if all were drunk, and that's when they made their mistake about old Bill Smiles, although he couldn't move. They would have given up the treasuries of the gulfs sooner than let men hear the prayers they said or guess their love for the goddess. It is the intimate secret of the sea.

The sailor paused. And, in my eagerness to hear

what lyrical or blasphemous thing those figureheads prayed by moonlight at midnight in the sea to the woman of marble who was a goddess to ships, I pressed on the sailor more of my Gorgondy wine that the gnomes so wickedly brew.

I should never have done it; but there he was sitting silent while the secret was almost mine. He took it moodily and drank a glass; and with the other glasses that he had he fell a prey to the villainy of the gnomes who brew this unbridled wine to no good end. His body leaned forward slowly, then fell on to the table, his face being sideways and full of wicked smile, and, saying very clearly the one word, "Hell," he became silent for ever with the secret he had from the sea.

The Compromise of the King of the Golden Isles

Dramatis Personae

THE KING OF THE GOLDEN ISLES: KING HAMARAN.
THE KING'S POLITICIAN.
THE AMBASSADOR OF THE EMPEROR.
THE EMPEROR'S SEEKER.
TWO PRIESTS OF THE ORDER OF THE SUN.
THE KING'S QUESTIONERS.
THE AMBASSADOR'S NUBIAN.
THE HERALD OF THE AMBASSADOR.
THE EMPEROR'S DWARF.
THE DEPUTY CUP-BEARER.
THE KING'S DOOM-BEARER.

THE KING'S POLITICIAN—A man has fled from the Emperor, and has taken refuge in your Majesty's Court in that part of it called holy.

THE KING—We must give him up to the Emperor.

POLITICIAN—To-day a spearsman came running from Eng-Bathai seeking the man who fled. He carries the barbed spear of one of the Emperor's seekers.

KING—We must give him up.

POLITICIAN—Moreover he has an edict from the Emperor demanding that the head of the man who fled be sent back to Eng-Bathai.

KING—Let it be sent.

POLITICIAN—Yet your Majesty is no vassal of the Emperor, who dwells at Eng-Bathai.

KING—We may not disobey the Imperial edict.

POLITICIAN—Yet——

KING—None hath dared to do it.

POLITICIAN—It is so long since any dared to do it that the Emperor mocks at kings. If your Majesty disobeyed him the Emperor would tremble.

KING—Ah.

POLITICIAN—The Emperor would say, "There is a great king. He defies me." And he would tremble strangely.

KING—Yet—if——

POLITICIAN—The Emperor would fear you.

KING—I would fain be a great king—yet——

POLITICIAN—You would win honour in his eyes.

KING—Yet is the Emperor terrible in his wrath. He was terrible in his wrath in the olden time.

POLITICIAN—The Emperor is old.

KING—This is a great affront that he places upon a king, to
    demand a man who has come to sanctuary in that
    part of my Court called holy.

POLITICIAN—It is a great affront.

> [*Enter the* SEEKER. *He abases himself.*

SEEKER—O King, I have come with my spear, seeking for
    one that fled the Emperor and has found sanc-
    tuary in your Court in that part called holy.

KING—It has not been the wont of the kings of my line to
    turn men from our sanctuary.

SEEKER—It is the Emperor's will.

KING—It is not *my* will.

SEEKER—Behold the Emperor's edict.

> [*The* KING *takes it. The* SEEKER *goes towards
> the door.*

SEEKER—I go to sit with my spear by the door of the place
    called holy.

> [*Exit* SEEKER.

KING—The edict, the edict. We must obey the edict.

POLITICIAN—The Emperor is old.

KING—True, we will defy him.

POLITICIAN—He will do nothing.

KING—And yet the edict.

POLITICIAN—It is of no importance.

KING—Hark. I will not disobey the Emperor. Yet will I not
    permit him to abuse the sanctuary of my Court.
    We will banish the man who fled from Eng-
    Bathai. [*To his* DOOM-BEARER.] Hither, the
    Doom-Bearer; take the black ivory spear, the
    wand of banishment, that lies on the left of my
    throne, and point it at the man that shelters in
    the holy place of my Court. Then show him the
    privy door behind the horns of the altar, so that
    he go safely hence and meet not the Emperor's
    seeker.

> [*The* DOOM-BEARER *bows and takes the spear
> on the flat of both his hands. The shaft is
> all black, but the head is of white ivory. It
> is blunt and clearly ceremonial. Exit.*

[*To* POLITICIAN.

Thus we shall be safe from the wrath of the Emperor, and the holy place of my Court will not be violate.

POLITICIAN—Had your Majesty scorned the Emperor it were better. He is old and durst not take vengeance.

KING—I have decided, and the man is banished.

[*A* HERALD *marches in and blows his trumpet.*

HERALD—The Ambassador of the Emperor.

[*Enter the* AMBASSADOR. *He bows to the King from his place near the door.*

KING—For what purpose to my Court from Eng-Bathai comes thus the Ambassador of the Emperor?

AMBASSADOR—I bring to the King's Majesty a gift from the great Emperor [AMBASSADOR *and his men bow*] who reigns in Eng-Bathai, the reward of obedience to his edict, a goblet of inestimable wine.

[*He signs and there enters a page bearing a goblet of glass. He has a pretty complexion and yellow hair falling as low as his chin and curling inwards. He wears a cerise belt round his tunic exactly matching the wine in the goblet he carries.*

He prays you drink it, and to know that it was made by vintners whose skill is lost, and stored in secret cellars over a hundred years; and that the vineyards whence it came have been long since whelmed by war, and only live now in legend and this wine.

KING—A gift, you say, for obedience.

AMBASSADOR—A gift from the old wine-gardens of the sun.

KING—How knew the Emperor that I had thus obeyed him?

AMBASSADOR—It has not been men's wont to disobey the Emperor.

KING—Yet if I have sheltered this man in the holy place of my Court?

AMBASSADOR—If that be so the Emperor bids you drink out of this golden goblet [*he signs and it is brought on by a bent and ugly dwarf*] and wishes you farewell.

KING—Farewell, you say?

AMBASSADOR—Farewell.

KING—What have you in the goblet?

AMBASSADOR—It is no common poison, but a thing so strange and deadly that the serpents of Lebutharna go in fear of it. Yea, travellers there hold high a goblet of this poison, at arm's length as they go. The serpents hide their heads for fear of it. Even so the travellers pass the desert safely, and come to Eng-Bathai.

KING—I have not sheltered this man.

AMBASSADOR—There is no need then for this Imperial gift.
[*He throws the liquid out of the goblet through the doorway on to the marble. A great steam goes up.*

KING—Neither have I ordered that his head be sent back to Eng-Bathai.

AMBASSADOR—Alas, for so rare a wine.
[*He pours it away.*

KING—I have banished him and he is safe. I have neither obeyed nor disobeyed.

AMBASSADOR—The Emperor therefore bids you choose the gift that he honours himself by sending to your Court.
[*He signs. Enter a massive* NUBIAN *with two cups.*

The Emperor bids you drink one of these cups.
[*The huge* NUBIAN *moves up close to the* KING *holding up the two cups on a tray.*
[*The* POLITICIAN *slinks off. Exit L.*

KING—The cups are strangely alike.

AMBASSADOR—Only one craftsman in the City of Smiths ever discerned a difference. The Emperor killed him, and now no one knows.

KING—The potions also are alike.

AMBASSADOR—Strangely alike. [*The* KING *hesitates.*] The Emperor bids you choose his gift and drink.

KING—The Emperor has poisoned the cups!

AMBASSADOR—You greatly wrong the Emperor. Only one cup is poisoned.

KING—You say that one is poisoned?

AMBASSADOR—Only one, O King! Who may say which?

KING—And what if I refuse to do this thing?

AMBASSADOR—There are tortures that the Emperor never names. They are not spoken of where the Emperor is. Yet the Emperor makes a sign and they are accomplished. He makes the sign with a certain one of his fingers.

KING (*half to himself*)—How wonderfully they have the look of wine.

AMBASSADOR—One is a wine scarcely less rare, scarcely less jubilant in the wits of man, than that which alas is lost.

> [*He glances towards the spot where he threw the other.*

KING—And the other?

AMBASSADOR—Who may say? It is the most treasured secret that the Emperor's poisoners guard.

KING—I will send for my butlers that are wise in wine and they shall smell the cups.

AMBASSADOR—Alas, but the Emperor's poisoners have added so wine-like a flavour to their most secret draught, that no man may tell by this means which is their work and which that inestimable wine.

KING—I will send for my tasters and they shall taste of the cups.

AMBASSADOR—Alas, so great a risk may not be run.

KING—Risks are the duty of a king's tasters.

AMBASSADOR—If they chanced to taste of the treasure of the Emperor's poisoners—well. But if they, or *any* man of common birth, were to taste of the wine that the Emperor sends only to kings, and even to kings but rarely, that were an affront to the Emperor's ancient wine that could not be permitted.

KING—It is surely permitted that I send for my priests, who tell by divination, having burnt strange herbs to the gods that guard the Golden Isles.

AMBASSADOR—It is permitted.

KING—Send for the priests.

KING (*mainly to himself*)—They shall discern. The priests shall make for me this dreadful choice. They shall burn herbs and discern it. (*To* AMBASSADOR.) My priests are very subtle. They worship the gods that guard the Golden Isles.

AMBASSADOR—The Emperor has other gods.

> [*Enter L. two priests of the Order of the Sun. Two acolytes follow. One carries a tripod and the other a gong.*
>
> [*The priests abase themselves and the acolytes bow. The* AMBASSADOR *stands with almost Mongolian calm by the door from which he has not moved since he entered.*
>
> [*The impassive* NUBIAN *stands motionless near the* KING, *holding up the cups on a tray.*

KING—The Emperor has honoured me with these two cups of wine that I may drink one of them to the grandeur of his throne. I bid you importune the gods that they may surely tell me which it were well to drink.

FIRST PRIEST—We will importune the gods with the savour of rarest spices. We will send up to them the odour of herbs they love. We will commune with them in silence and they shall answer our thoughts, when they snuff the savour of the smoke of the burning on the tripod that is sacred to the Sun.

> [*The calm of the* AMBASSADOR *and the impassivity of the* NUBIAN *grow ominous. The two priests hang over the tripod. They cast*

> *herbs upon it. They pass their hands over it. The herbs begin to smoulder. A smoke goes up. The priests bend over the smoke. Presently they step back from it.*

FIRST PRIEST—The gods sleep.

KING—They sleep! The gods that guard the Golden Isles?

FIRST PRIEST—The gods sleep.

KING—Importune them as never before. I will make sacrifice of many sheep. I will give emeralds to the Monks of the Sun.

> *The second acolyte moves nearer to the tripod and beats listlessly on his great gong at about the pace of a great clock striking slowly.*

FIRST PRIEST—We will importune the gods as never before.

> *They heap up more herbs and spices. The smoke grows thicker and thicker. It streams upwards. They hover about it as before. At a sign the gong ceases.*

The gods have spoken.

KING—What is their message?

FIRST PRIEST—Drink of the cup upon the Nubian's left.

KING—Ah. My gods defend me.

> *He seizes the cup boldly. He looks straight at the AMBASSADOR, whose face remains expressionless, merely watching. He lifts the cup upon the Nubian's left a little up from the tray.*

> *He glances towards the priests.*

> *Suddenly he starts. He has seen a strange expression upon the face of the priest. He puts the cup down. He strides a step nearer and looks at his face.*

PRIEST!—Priest!——What is that look in your eyes?

FIRST PRIEST—O King, I know not. I have given the message of the gods.

> *The KING continues to search out his face.*

KING—I mistrust it.

FIRST PRIEST—It is the message of the gods.

KING—I will drink of the other cup!

> [*The* KING *steps back to his place in the front of his throne where the Nubian stands beside him. He takes the cup upon the Nubian's right. He gazes at the priest. He looks round at the Ambassador, but sees nothing in that watchful, expressionless face.*

> [*He glances sidelong at the priest, then drinks, draining the cup at some length. He puts it down in silence. The face of the Ambassador and the whole bulk of the Nubian remain motionless.*

KING—An inestimable wine!

AMBASSADOR—It is the Emperor's joy.

KING—Send for my Questioners.

> [*There are weird whistles. Two dark men run on in loin clothes.*

Ask these two priests the Seven Questions.

> [*The* QUESTIONERS *run nimbly up to the two priests and lead them away by the arm.*

THE TWO ACOLYTES—O, O, O. Oh, oh.

> [*They show extreme horror. The* AMBASSADOR *bows to the King.*

KING—You do not leave us at once?

AMBASSADOR—I go back to the Emperor, whom it is happiness to obey, and length of days.

> [*He bows and walks away. The* HERALD *marches out, then the* AMBASSADOR; *the* PAGE, *the* DWARF *and the* NUBIAN *follow.*

> [*Exeunt.*

> [*The* HERALD *is heard blowing upon his trumpet the same notes as when he entered, one merry bar of music.*

> [*The tray and two precious cups, one empty and the other full, are left glittering near the* KING.

KING (*looking at cups*)—Those are rare emeralds that glisten there! Yet an evil gift. (*To the moaning acolytes.*) Be silent! Your priests sinned strangely.

[*The acolytes continue to moan.*

[*Enter one of the* QUESTIONERS. *He has sweat on his face and his hair has become damp and unkempt.*

QUESTIONER—We have asked the Seven Questions.

KING—Well?

QUESTIONER—They have not answered.

KING—Not answered!

QUESTIONER—Neither man has confessed.

KING—Oho! Do I keep Questioners that bring me no answers?

QUESTIONER—We questioned them to the uttermost.

KING—And neither man confessed?

QUESTIONER—They would not confess.

KING—Ask them the Supreme Question.

[*The acolytes break out into renewed moaning.*

QUESTIONER—It shall be asked, O King.

[*Exit* QUESTIONER. *The acolytes moan on.*

KING—They would have made me drink of a poisoned cup. I say there is poison in that cup. Your priests would have had me drink it. (*The acolytes only answer by moans.*) Bid them confess. Bid them confess their crime and why it was done, and the Supreme Question shall be spared them. (*The acolytes only answer by moans.*) Strange! They have done strangely. (*To acolytes.*) Why has your priest spoken falsely? (*The acolytes only moan.*) Why has he spoken falsely in the name of the gods? (*The acolytes moan on.*) Be silent! Be silent! May I not question whom I will? (*To himself*). They prophesied falsely in the name of the gods.

[*Enter the* QUESTIONERS.

FIRST QUESTIONER—The Supreme Question is asked.

[*The acolytes suddenly cease moaning.*

KING—Well?

FIRST QUESTIONER—They would not answer.

KING—They would not answer the Supreme Question?

FIRST QUESTIONER—They spoke at last, but they would not answer the question. They would not confess.

KING—What said they at last?

FIRST QUESTIONER—O, the King's Majesty, they but spake idly.

KING—What said they?

FIRST QUESTIONER—O, the King's Majesty, they said nought fitting.

KING—They muttered so that no man heard them clearly?

FIRST QUESTIONER—They spake. But it was not fitting.

KING—Did they speak of small things happening long ago?

FIRST QUESTIONER—O, the King's Majesty, it was not fitting.

KING—What said they? Speak!

FIRST QUESTIONER—The man you gave to me, O King, said: "No man that knew the counsels of the gods, who alone see future things would say the gods advised King Hamaran ill when they bade him drink out of a poisoned cup." Then I put the question straightly and he died.

KING—The gods! He said it was the gods! . . . And the other?

SECOND QUESTIONER—He also said the same, O the King's Majesty.

KING—Both said the same. They were questioned in different chambers?

FIRST QUESTIONER—In different chambers, O King. I questioned mine in the Red Chamber.

KING (*to* SECOND QUESTIONER)—And yours?

SECOND QUESTIONER—In the Chamber of Rats.

KING—Begone!

[*Exeunt* QUESTIONERS.

So . . . It *was* the gods.

[*The acolytes are crouched upon the floor. He does not notice them since they ceased to moan.*

The gods! With what dark and dreadful thing have they clouded the future? Well, I will face it! But what is it? Is it one of those things a strong man can bear? Or is it———?

The future is more terrible than the grave, that has its one secret only.

No man, he said, could say that the gods had advised me ill when they bade me drink out of a poisoned cup.

What have the gods seen? What dreadful work have they overlooked where Destiny sits alone, making evil years?

The gods, he said, who alone see future things.

Yes, I have known men who never were warned by the gods, and did not drink poison, and came upon evil days, suddenly like a ship upon rocks no mariner knows.

Yes, poison to some of *them* would have been very precious.

The gods have warned me and I have not hearkened, and must go on alone: must enter that strange country of the future whose paths are so dark to man . . . to meet a doom there that the gods have seen.

The gods have seen it! How shall I thwart the gods? How fight against the shapers of the hills? Would that I had been warned. Would I had heeded when they bade me drink of the cup the Ambassador said was poisoned.

> [*Far off is heard that merry bar of music blown by the* AMBASSADOR'S HERALD *on his horn.*]

Is it too late?

There it stands yet with its green emeralds winking.

> [*He clutches it and looks down into it.*

How like to wine it is, which is full of dreams. It is silent and dreamy like the gods, whose dreams we are.

Only a moment in their deathless minds: then the dream passes.

[*He lifts up his arm and drinks it seated upon his throne with his head back and the great cup before his face. The audience begin to wonder when he will put it down. Still he remains in the attitude of a drinker. The acolytes begin to peer eagerly. Still he remains upright with the great cup to his lips. The acolytes patter away and the* KING *is left alone.*

[*Enter the* KING'S POLITICIAN *hurriedly. He goes up to the* KING *and seizes his right arm and tries to drag the cup away from his lips, but the* KING *is rigid and his arm cannot be moved. He steps back lifting up his hands.*

POLITICIAN—Oh·h!

[*Exit. You hear him announcing solemnly*

King Hamaran . . . is dead!

[*A murmur is heard of men, at first mournful. It grows louder and louder and then breaks into these clear words.*

Zarabardes is King! Zarabardes is King. Rejoice! Rejoice! Zarabardes is King! Zarabardes! Zarabardes! Zarabardes!

CURTAIN.

Tales of Far Away

Editor's Note

LORD DUNSANY wrote stories of many kinds, laid in a variety of settings. In this second section I have gathered together some examples of those which find their locales in the fabulous Eastern realms between the "Fields We Know" and "the World's Edge"—a shadowy mid-region contiguous with the Waking World of Everyday on one side and bordering Faërie on the other.

Also included here is another of his plays, "The Queen's Enemies." The occasion of its genesis was a chance trip up the Nile on a tourist steamer named *Nitocris*. (Lord and Lady Dunsany had arrived in Egypt in late November, 1908, and were taking the steamer to Aswan.) During the trip, Dunsany began thinking about the boat's namesake, that vengeful murderess-queen of the Sixth Dynasty whose story is told by Herodotus in *The Histories*.

Five years later he was to sit down and actually write "The Queen's Enemies." It was first produced at the Neighborhood Playhouse in New York on November 14, 1916.

L.C.

The House of the Sphinx

When I came to the House of the Sphinx it was already dark. They made me eagerly welcome. And I, in spite of the deed, was glad of any shelter from that ominous wood. I saw at once that there had been a deed, although a cloak did all that a cloak may do to conceal it. The mere uneasiness of the welcome made me suspect that cloak.

The Sphinx was moody and silent. I had not come to pry into the secrets of Eternity nor to investigate the Sphinx's private life, and so had little to say and few questions to ask; but to whatever I did say she remained morosely indifferent. It was clear that either she suspected me of being in search of the secrets of one of her gods, or of being boldly inquisitive about her traffic with Time, or else she was darkly absorbed with brooding upon the deed.

I saw soon enough that there was another than me to welcome; I saw it from the hurried way that they glanced from the door to the deed and back to the door again. And it was clear that the welcome was to be a bolted door. But such bolts, and such a door! Rust and decay and fungus had been there far too long, and it was not a barrier any longer than would keep out even a determined wolf. And it seemed to be something worse than a wolf that they feared.

A little later on I gathered from what they said that some imperious and ghastly thing was looking for the Sphinx, and that something that had happened had made its arrival certain. It appeared that they had slapped the Sphinx to vex her out of her apathy in order that she should pray to one of her gods, whom she had littered in the house of Time; but her moody silence was invincible, and her apathy Oriental, ever since the deed had happened. And when they found that they could not make her pray, there was nothing for them to do but to pay little useless attentions to the rusty lock of the door, and to look at the deed and wonder, and even pretend to hope, and to say that after all it might not bring that destined thing from the forest, which no one named.

It may be said I had chosen a gruesome house, but not if I had described the forest from which I came, and I was in need of any spot wherein I could rest my mind from the thought of it.

I wondered very much what thing would come from the forest on account of the deed; and having seen that forest—as you, gentle reader, have not—I had the advantage of knowing that anything might come. It was useless to ask the Sphinx—she seldom reveals things, like her paramour Time (the gods take after her), and while this mood was on her, rebuff was certain. So I quietly began to oil the lock of the door. And as soon as they saw this simple act I won their confidence. It was not that my work was of any use—it should have been done long before; but they saw that my interest was given for the moment to the thing that they thought vital. They clustered round me then. They asked me what I thought of the door, and whether I had seen better, and whether I had seen worse; and I told them about all the doors I knew, and said that the doors of the baptistery in Florence were better doors, and the doors made by a certain firm of builders in London were worse. And then I asked them what it was that was coming after the Sphinx because of the deed. And at first they would not say, and I stopped oiling the door; and then they said that it was the arch-inquisitor of the forest, who is investigator and avenger of all silvestrian things; and from all that they said about him it seemed to me that this person was quite white, and was a kind of madness that would settle down quite blankly upon the place, a kind of mist in which reason could not live; and it was the fear of this that made them fumble nervously at the lock of that rotten door; but with the Sphinx it was not so much fear as sheer prophecy.

The hope that they tried to hope was well enough in its way, but I did not share it; it was clear that the thing that they feared was the corollary of the deed— one saw that more by the resignation upon the face of the Sphinx than by their sorry anxiety for the door.

The wind soughed, and the great tapers flared, and their obvious fear and the silence of the Sphinx grew more than ever a part of the atmosphere, and bats went restlessly through the gloom of the wind that beat the tapers low.

Then a few things screamed far off, then a little nearer, and something was coming towards us, laughing hideously. I hastily gave a prod to the door that they guarded; my finger sank right into the mouldering wood —there was not a chance of holding it. I had not leisure to observe their fright; I thought of the back-door, for the forest was better than this; only the Sphinx was absolutely calm, her prophecy was made and she seemed to have seen her doom, so that no new thing could perturb her.

But by mouldering rungs of ladders as old as Man, by slippery edges of the dreaded abyss, with an ominous dizziness about my heart and a feeling of horror in the soles of my feet, I clambered from tower to tower till I found the door that I sought; and it opened on to one of the upper branches of a huge and sombre pine, down which I climbed on to the floor of the forest. And I was glad to be back again in the forest from which I had fled.

And the Sphinx in her menaced house—I know not how she fared—whether she gazes for ever, discon-solate, at the deed, remembering only in her smitten mind, at which little boys now leer, that she once knew well those things at which man stands aghast; or whether in the end she crept away, and clambering horribly from abyss to abyss, came at last to higher things, and is wise and eternal still. For who knows of madness whether it is divine or whether it be of the pit?

Blagdaross

On a waste place strewn with bricks in the outskirts of a town twilight was falling. A star or two appeared over the smoke, and distant windows lit mysterious lights. The stillness deepened and the loneliness. Then all the outcast things that are silent by day found voices.

An old cork spoke first. He said: "I grew in Andalusian woods, but never listened to the idle songs of Spain. I only grew strong in the sunlight waiting for my destiny. One day the merchants came and took us all away and carried us all along the shore of the sea, piled high on the backs of donkeys, and in a town by the sea they made me into the shape that I am now. One day they sent me northward to Provence, and there I fulfilled my destiny. For they set me as guard over the bubbling wine, and I faithfully stood sentinel for twenty years. For the first few years in the bottle that I guarded the wine slept, dreaming of Provence; but as the years went on he grew stronger and stronger, until at last whenever a man went by the wine would put out all his might against me, saying: 'Let me go free; let me go free!' And every year his strength increased, and he grew more clamorous when men went by, but never availed to hurl me from my post. But when I had powerfully held him for twenty years they brought him to the banquet and took me from my post, and the wine arose rejoicing and leapt through the veins of men and exalted their souls within them till they stood up in their places and sang Provençal songs. But me they cast away—me that had been sentinel for twenty years, and was still as strong and staunch as when first I went on guard. Now I am an outcast in a cold northern city, who once have known the Andalusian skies and guarded long ago Provençal suns that swam in the heart of the rejoicing wine."

An unstruck match that somebody had dropped spoke next. "I am a child of the sun," he said, "and an enemy of cities; there is more in my heart than you know of. I am a brother of Etna and Stromboli; I have fires lurking in me that will one day rise up beautiful and strong. We will not go into servitude on any hearth nor work machines for our food, but we will take our own food where we find it on that day when we are strong. There are wonderful children in my heart whose faces shall be more lively than the rainbow; they shall make a compact with the North wind, and he shall lead them forth; all shall be black behind them and black above them, and there shall be nothing beautiful in the world but them; they shall seize upon the earth and it shall be theirs, and nothing shall stop them but our old enemy the sea."

Then an old broken kettle spoke, and said: "I am the friend of cities. I sit among the slaves upon the hearth, the little flames that have been fed with coal. When the slaves dance behind the iron bars I sit in the middle of the dance and sing and make our masters glad. And I make songs about the comfort of the cat, and about the malice that is towards her in the heart of the dog, and about the crawling of the baby, and about the ease that is in the lord of the house when we brew the good brown tea; and sometimes when the house is very warm and slaves and masters are glad, I rebuke the hostile winds that prowl about the world."

And then there spoke the piece of an old cord. "I was made in a place of doom, and doomed men made my fibres, working without hope. Therefore there came a grimness into my heart, so that I never let anything go free when once I was set to bind it. Many a thing have I bound relentlessly for months and for years; for I used to come coiling into warehouses where the great boxes lay all open to the air, and one of them would be suddenly closed up, and my fearful strength would be set on him like a curse, and if his timbers groaned when first I seized them, or if they creaked aloud in the lonely night, thinking of woodlands out of which they came, then I only gripped them tighter still, for the poor useless hate is in my soul of those that made me in the place of doom. Yet, for all the things that my prison-clutch has held, the last work that I did was to set something free. I lay idle one night in the gloom on the warehouse floor. Nothing stirred there, and even the spider slept. Towards midnight a great flock of echoes suddenly leapt up from the wooden planks and circled round the roof. A man was coming towards me all alone. And as he came his soul was reproaching him, and I saw that there was a great trouble between the man and his soul, for his soul would not let him be, but went on reproaching him.

"Then the man saw me and said, 'This at least will not fail me.' When I heard him say this about me, I determined that whatever he might require of me it should be done to the uttermost. And as I made this determination in my unaltering heart, he picked me up and stood on an empty box that I should have bound on the morrow, and tied one end of me to a dark rafter; and the knot was carelessly tied, because his soul was reproaching him all the while continually and giving him no ease. Then he made the other end of me into a noose, but when the man's soul saw this it stopped reproaching the man, and cried out to him hurriedly, and besought him to be at peace with it and to do nothing sudden; but the man went on with his work, and put the noose down over his face and underneath his chin, and the soul screamed horribly.

"Then the man kicked the box away with his foot, and the moment he did this I knew that my strength was not great enough to hold him; but I remembered that he had said I would not fail him, and I put all my grim vigour into my fibres and held him by sheer will. Then the soul shouted to me to give way, but I said:

" 'No; you vexed the man.'

"Then it screamed to me to leave go of the rafter, and already I was slipping, for I only held on to it by a careless knot, but I gripped with my prison grip and said:

" 'You vexed the man.'

"And very swiftly it said other things to me, but I answered not; and at last the soul that vexed the man that had trusted me flew away and left him at peace. I was never able to bind things any more, for every one of my fibres was worn and wrenched, and even my relentless heart was weakened by the struggle. Very soon afterwards I was thrown out here. I have done my work."

So they spoke among themselves, but all the while there loomed above them the form of an old rocking-horse complaining bitterly. He said: "I am Blagdaross. Woe is me that I should lie now an outcast among these worthy but little people. Alas! for the days that are gathered, and alas for the Great One that was a master and a soul to me, whose spirit is now shrunken and can never know me again, and no more ride abroad on knightly quests. I was Bucephalus when he was Alexander, and carried him victorious as far as Ind. I encountered dragons with him when he was St. George, I was the horse of Roland fighting for Christendom, and was often Rosinante. I fought in tournays and went errant upon quests, and met Ulysses and the heroes and the fairies. Or late in the evening, just before the lamps in the nursery were put out, he would suddenly mount me, and we would gallop through Africa. There, we would pass by night through tropic forests, and come upon dark rivers sweeping by, all gleaming with the eyes of crocodiles, where the hippopotamus floated down with the stream, and mysterious craft loomed suddenly out of the dark and furtively passed away. And when we had passed through the forest lit by the fireflies we would come to the open plains, and gallop onwards with scarlet flamingoes flying along beside us through the lands of dusky kings, with golden crowns upon their heads and sceptres in their hands, who came running out of their palaces to see us pass. Then I would wheel suddenly, and the dust flew up from my four hoofs as I turned and we galloped home again, and my master was put to bed. And again he would ride abroad on another day till we came to magical fortresses guarded by wizardry and overthrew the dragons at the gate, and ever came back with a princess fairer than the sea.

"But my master began to grow larger in his body and smaller in his soul, and then he rode more seldom upon quests. At last he saw gold and never came again, and I was cast out here among these little people."

But while the rocking-horse was speaking two boys stole away, unnoticed by their parents, from a house on the edge of the waste place, and were coming across it looking for adventures. One of them carried a broom, and when he saw the rocking-horse he said nothing, but broke off the handle from the broom and thrust it between his braces and his shirt on the left side. Then he mounted the rocking-horse, and drawing forth the broomstick, which was sharp and spiky at the end, said, "Saladin is in this desert with all his paynims, and I am Cœur de Lion." After a while the other boy said: "Now let me kill Saladin too." But Blagdaross in his wooden heart, that exulted with thoughts of battle, said. "I am Blagdaross yet!"

The Lonely Idol

I had from a friend an old outlandish stone, a little swine-faced idol to whom no one prayed.

And when I saw his melancholy case as he sat cross-legged at receipt of prayer, holding a little scourge that the years had broken (and no one heeded the scourge and no one prayed and no one came with squealing sacrifice; and he had been a god), then I took pity on the little forgotten thing and prayed to it as perhaps they prayed long since, before the coming of the strange dark ships, and humbled myself and said:

"O idol, idol of the hard pale stone, invincible to the years, O scourge-holder, give ear for behold I pray.

"O little pale-green image whose wanderings are from far, know thou that here in Europe and in other lands near by, too soon there pass from us the sweets and song and the lion strength of youth: too soon do their cheeks fade, their hair grow grey and our beloved die; too brittle is beauty, too far off is fame and the years are gathered too soon; there are leaves, leaves falling, everywhere falling; there is autumn among men, autumn and reaping; failure there is, struggle, dying and weeping, and all that is beautiful hath not remained but is even as the glory of morning upon the water.

"Even our memories are gathered too with the sound of the ancient voices, the pleasant ancient voices that come to our ears no more; the very gardens of our childhood fade, and there dims with the speed of the years even the mind's own eye.

"O be not any more the friend of Time, for the silent hurry of his malevolent feet have trodden down what's fairest; I almost hear the whimper of the years running behind him hound-like, and it takes few to tear us.

"All that is beautiful he crushes down as a big man tramples daisies, all that is fairest. How very fair are the little children of men. It is autumn with all the world, and the stars weep to see it.

"Therefore no longer be the friend of Time, who will not let us be, and be not good to him but pity us, and let lovely things live on for the sake of our tears."

Thus prayed I out of compassion one windy day to the snout-faced idol to whom no one kneeled.

An Archive of the
Older Mysteries

It is told in the Archive of the Older Mysteries of China that one of the house of Tlang was cunning with sharpened iron and he went to the green jade mountains and carved a green jade god. And this was in the cycle of the Dragon, the seventy-eighth year.

And for nearly a hundred years men doubted the green jade god, and then they worshipped him for a thousand years; and after that they doubted him again, and the green jade god made a miracle and whelmed the green jade mountains, sinking them down one evening at sunset into the earth so that there is only a marsh where the green jade mountains were. And the marsh is full of the lotus.

By the side of this lotus marsh, just as it glitters at evening, walks Li La Ting, the Chinese girl, to bring the cows home; she goes behind them singing of the river Lo Lang Ho. And thus she sings of the river, even of Lo Lang Ho: she sings that he is indeed of all rivers the greatest, born of more ancient mountains than even the wise men know, swifter than hares, more deep than the sea, the master of other rivers perfumed even as roses and fairer than the sapphires around the neck of a prince. And then she would pray to the river Lo Lang Ho, master of rivers and rival of the heaven at dawn, to bring her down in a boat of light bamboo a lover rowing out of the inner land in a garment of yellow silk with turquoises at his waist, young and merry and idle, with a face as yellow as gold and a ruby in his cap with lanterns shining at dusk.

Thus she would pray of an evening to the river Lo Lang Ho as she went behind the cows at the edge of the lotus marshes and the green jade god under the lotus marshes was jealous of the lover that the maiden Li La Ting would pray for of an evening to the river Lo Lang Ho, and he cursed the river after the manner of gods and turned it into a narrow and evil smelling stream.

And all this happened a thousand years ago, and Lo Lang Ho is but a reproach among travellers and the glory of that great river is forgotten, and what became of the maiden no tale saith though all men think she became a goddess of jade to sit and smile at a lotus on a lotus carven of stone by the side of the green jade god far under the marshes upon the peaks of the mountains, but women know that her ghost still haunts the lotus marshes on glittering evenings, singing of Lo Lang Ho.

The Loot of Loma

Coming back laden with the loot of Loma, the four
tall men looked earnestly to the right; to the left they
durst not, for the precipice there that had been with
them so long went sickly down on to a bank of clouds,
and how much farther below that only their fears could
say.

Loma lay smoking, a city of ruin, behind them, all
its defenders dead; there was no one left to pursue
them, and yet their Indian instincts told them that all
was scarcely well. They had gone three days along that
narrow ledge: mountain quite smooth, incredible, above
them, and precipice as smooth and as far below. It was
chilly there in the mountains; at night a stream or a
wind in the gloom of the chasm below them went like
a whisper; the stillness of all things else began to wear
the nerve—an enemy's howl would have braced them;
they began to wish their perilous path were wider, they
began to wish that they had not sacked Loma.

Had that path been any wider the sacking of Loma
must indeed have been harder for them, for the citizens
must have fortified the city but that the awful narrow-
ness of that ten-league pass of the hills had made their
crag-surrounded city secure. And at last an Indian had
said, "Come, let us sack it." Grimly they laughed in the
wigwams. Only the eagles, they said, had ever seen it,
its hoard of emeralds and its golden gods; and one had
said he would reach it, and they answered, "Only the
eagles."

It was Laughing Face who said it, and who gathered
thirty braves and led them into Loma with their toma-
hawks and their bows; there were only four left now,

but they had the loot of Loma on a mule. They had four golden gods, a hundred emeralds, fifty-two rubies, a large silver gong, two sticks of malachite with amethyst handles for holding incense at religious feasts, four beakers one foot high, each carved from a rose-quartz crystal; a little coffer carved out of two diamonds, and (had they but known it) the written curse of a priest. It was written on parchment in an unknown tongue, and had been slipped in with the loot by a dying hand.

From either end of that narrow, terrible ledge the third night was closing in; it was dropping down on them from the heights of the mountain and slipping up to them out of the abyss, the third night since Loma blazed and they had left it. Three more days of tramping should bring them in triumph home, and yet their instincts said that all was scarcely well. We who sit at home and draw the blinds and shut the shutters as soon as night appears, who gather round the fire when the wind is wild, who pray at regular seasons and in familiar shrines, know little of the demoniac look of night when it is filled with curses of false, infuriated gods. Such a night was this. Though in the heights the fleecy clouds were idle, yet the wind was stirring mournfully in the abyss and moaning as it stirred, unhappily at first and full of sorrow; but as day turned away from that awful path a very definite menace entered its voice which fast grew louder and louder, and night came on with a long howl. Shadows repeatedly passed over the stars, and then a mist fell swiftly, as though there were something suddenly to be done and utterly to be hidden, as in very truth there was.

And in the chill of that mist the four tall men prayed to their totems, the whimsical wooden figures that stood so far away, watching the pleasant wigwams; the firelight even now would be dancing over their faces, while there would come to their ears delectable tales of war. They halted upon the pass and prayed, and waited for any sign. For a man's totem may be in the likeness perhaps of an otter, and a man may pray, and if his totem be placable and watching over his man a noise may be heard at once like the noise that the otter makes, though it be but a stone that falls on another stone; and the noise is a sign. The four men's totems that stood so far away were in the likeness of the coney, the bear, the heron, and the lizard. They waited, and no sign came. With all the noises of the wind in the abyss, no noise was like the thump that the coney makes, nor the bear's growl, nor the heron's screech, nor the rustle of the lizard in the reeds.

It seemed that the wind was saying something over and over again, and that that thing was evil. They prayed again to their totems, and no sign came. And then they knew that there was some power that night that was prevailing against the pleasant carvings on painted poles of wood with the firelight on their faces so far away. Now it was clear that the wind was saying something, some very, very dreadful thing in a tongue that they did not know. They listened, but they could not tell what it said. Nobody could have said from seeing their faces how much the four tall men desired the wigwams again, desired the camp-fire and the tales of war and the benignant totems that listened and smiled in the dusk: Nobody could have seen how well they knew that this was no common night or wholesome mist.

When at last no answer came nor any sign from their totems, they pulled out of the bag those golden gods that Loma gave not up except in flames and when all her men were dead. They had large ruby eyes and emerald tongues. They set them down upon that mountain pass, the cross-legged idols with their emerald tongues; and having placed between them a few decent yards, as it seemed meet there should be between gods and men, they bowed them down and prayed in their desperate straits in that dank, ominous night to the gods they had wronged, for it seemed that there was a vengeance upon the hills and that they would scarce escape, as the wind knew well. And the gods laughed, all four, and wagged their emerald tongues; the Indians saw them, though the night had fallen and though the mist was low. The four tall men leaped up at once from their knees and would have left the gods upon the pass but that they feared some hunter of their tribe might one day find them and say of Laughing Face, "He fled and left behind his golden gods," and sell the gold and come with his wealth to the wigwams and be greater than Laughing Face and his three men. And then they would have cast the gods away, down the abyss, with their eyes and their emerald tongues, but they knew that enough already they had wronged Loma's gods, and feared that vengeance enough was waiting them on the hills. So they packed them back in the bag on the frightened mule, the bag that held the curse they knew nothing of, and so pushed on into the menacing night. Till midnight they plodded on and would not sleep; grimmer and grimmer grew the look of the night, and the wind more full of meaning, and the mule knew and trembled, and it seemed that the wind knew, too, as did the instincts of those four tall men, though they could not reason it out, try how they would.

And though the squaws waited long where the pass winds out of the mountains, near where the wigwams are upon the plains, the wigwams and the totems and the fire, and though they watched by day, and for many nights uttered familiar calls, still did they never see those four tall men emerge out of the mountains any more, even though they prayed to their totems upon their painted poles; but the curse in the mystical writing that they had unknown in their bag worked there on that lonely pass six leagues from the ruins of Loma, and nobody can tell us what it was.

The Last Dream of
Bwona Khubla

From steaming lowlands down by the equator, where monstrous orchids blow, where beetles big as mice sit on the tent-ropes, and fireflies glide about by night like little moving stars, the travelers went three days through forests of cactus till they came to the open plains where the oryx are.

And glad they were when they came to the water-hole, where only one white man had gone before, which the natives know as the camp of Bwona Khubla, and found the water there.

It lies three days from the nearest other water, and when Bwona Khubla had gone there three years ago, what with malaria with which he was shaking all over, and what with disgust at finding the water-hole dry, he had decided to die there, and in that part of the world such decisions are always fatal. In any case he was overdue to die, but hitherto his amazing resolution, and that terrible strength of character that so astounded his porters, had kept him alive and moved his safari on.

He had had a name no doubt, some common name such as hangs as likely as not over scores of shops in London; but that had gone long ago, and nothing identified his memory now to distinguish it from the memories of all the other dead but "Bwona Khubla," the name the Kikuyus gave him.

There is no doubt that he was a fearful man, a man that was dreaded still for his personal force when his arm was no longer able to lift the kiboko, when all his men knew he was dying, and to this day though he is dead.

Though his temper was embittered by malaria and

the equatorial sun, nothing impaired his will, which remained a compulsive force to the very last, impressing itself upon all, and after the last, from what the Kikuyus say. The country must have had powerful laws that drove Bwona Khubla out, whatever country it was.

On the morning of the day that they were to come to the camp of Bwona Khubla all the porters came to the travelers' tents asking for dow. Dow is the white man's medicine, that cures all evils; the nastier it tastes, the better it is. They wanted dow this morning to keep away devils, for they were near the place where Bwona Khubla died.

The travelers gave them quinine.

By sunset they came to Campini Bwona Khubla and found water there. Had they not found water many of them must have died, yet none felt any gratitude to the place, it seemed too ominous, too full of a doom, too much harassed almost by unseen, irresistible things.

And all the natives came again for dow as soon as the tents were pitched, to protect them from the last dreams of Bwona Khubla; which they say had stayed behind when the last safari left taking Bwona Khubla's body back to the edge of civilization to show to the white men there that they had not killed him, for the white men might not know that they durst not kill Bwona Khubla.

And the travelers gave them more quinine, so much being bad for their nerves, and that night by the camp-fires there was no pleasant talk, all talking at once of meat they had eaten and cattle that each one owned, but a gloomy silence hung by every fire and the little canvas shelters. They told the white men that Bwona Khubla's city, of which he had thought at the last (and where the natives believed he was once a king), of which he had raved till the loneliness rang with his raving, had settled down all about them; and they were afraid, for it was so strange a city, and wanted more dow. And the two travelers gave them more quinine, for they saw real fear in their faces, and knew they might run away and leave them alone in that place, that they, too, had come to fear with an almost equal dread, though they knew not why. And as the night wore on their feeling of boding deepened, although they had shared three bottles or so of champagne that they meant to keep for days when they killed a lion.

This is the story that each of those two men tell, and which their porters corroborate, but then a Kikuyu will always say whatever he thinks is expected of him.

The travelers were both in bed and trying to sleep but not able to do so because of an ominous feeling. That mournfullest of all the cries of the wild, the hyæna like a damned soul lamenting, strangely enough had ceased. The night wore on to the hour when Bwona Khubla had died three or four years ago, dreaming and raving of "his city"; and in the hush a sound softly arose, like a wind at first, then like the roar of beasts, then unmistakably the sound of motors—motors and motor busses.

And then they saw, clearly and unmistakably they say, in that lonely desolation where the equator comes up out of the forest and climbs over jagged hills—they say they saw London.

There could have been no moon that night, but they say there was a multitude of stars. Mists had come rolling up at evening about the pinnacles of unexplored red peaks that clustered round the camp. But they say the mist must have cleared later on; at any rate they swear they could see London, see it and hear the roar of it. Both say they saw it not as they knew it at all, not debased by hundreds of thousands of lying advertisements, but transfigured, all its houses magnificent, its chimneys rising grandly into pinnacles, its vast squares full of the most gorgeous trees, transfigured and yet London.

Its windows were warm and happy, shining at night, the lamps in their long rows welcomed you, the public-houses were gracious jovial places; yet it was London.

They could smell the smells of London, hear London songs, and yet it was never the London that they knew; it was as though they had looked on some strange woman's face with the eyes of her lover. For of all the towns of the earth or cities of song; of all the spots there be, unhallowed or hallowed, it seemed to those two men then that the city they saw was of all places the most to be desired by far. They say a barrel organ played quite near them, they say a coster was singing, they admit that he was singing out of tune, they admit a cockney accent, and yet they say that that song had in it something that no earthly song had ever had before, and both men say that they would have wept but that there was a feeling about their heart-strings that was far too deep for tears. They believe that the longing of this masterful man, that was able to rule a safari by a glance of his eye, and could terrify natives without raising a hand, had been so strong at the last that it had impressed itself deeply upon nature and had caused a mirage that may not fade wholly away, perhaps for several years.

I tried to establish by questions the truth or reverse of this story, but the two men's tempers had been so spoiled by Africa that they were not up to a cross-examination. They would not even say if their camp-fires were still burning. They say that they saw the London lights all round them from eleven o'clock till midnight, they could hear London voices and the sound of the traffic clearly; and over all, a little misty perhaps, but unmistakably London, arose the great metropolis.

About midnight London quivered a little and grew more indistinct, the sound of the traffic began to dwindle away, voices seemed farther off, ceased altogether, and all was quiet once more where the mirage shimmered and faded, and a bull rhinoceros coming down through the stillness snorted, and watered at the Carlton Club.

The Queen's Enemies

Dramatis Personae

THE QUEEN.
ACKAZÁRPSES, *her handmaid.*
PRINCE RHÁDAMANDÁSPES.
PRINCE ZOPHERNES.
THE PRIEST OF HORUS.
THE KING OF THE FOUR COUNTRIES.
THE TWIN DUKES OF ETHIOPIA.

THARNI
THÁRRABAS } *Slaves.*
HARLEE

SLAVES.
SCENE:—*An underground temple in Egypt.*
TIME:—*The Sixth Dynasty.*

[The stage is in two parts. Right—a staircase descending to a door. Left—an underground temple into which the door opens.]

[The Curtain rises on darkness in both parts of the stage.]

[Two Slaves appear with tapers on the steps. As they go down the steps, they light the torches that are clamped against the wall, with their tapers. Afterwards when they come to the temple they light the torches there till they are all lit. There is a table prepared for a banquet in the temple and a sewer-like grating in the middle of a wall. The two Slaves are Tharni and Thárrabas.]

THÁRRABAS—Is it much further, Tharni?

THARNI—I think not, Thárrabas.

THÁRRABAS—A dank and terrible place.

THARNI—It is not much further.

THÁRRABAS—Why does the Queen banquet in so fearful a place?

THARNI—I know not. She banquets with her enemies.

THÁRRABAS—In the land from which I was taken we do not banquet with our enemies.

THARNI—No? The Queen will banquet with her enemies.

THÁRRABAS—Why? Know you why?

THARNI—It is the way of the Queen.

[Silence.]

THÁRRABAS—The door, Tharni, we have come to the door!

THARNI—Yes, that's the Temple.

THÁRRABAS—Surely a grim place.

THARNI—The banquet is prepared. We light these torches, that is all.

THÁRRABAS—Unto whom is it holy?

THARNI—They say to the Nile once. I know not unto whom it is holy now.

THÁRRABAS—So Nile has left it?

THARNI—They say they worship him in this place no longer.

THÁRRABAS—And if I were holy Nile I also would stay up there [*pointing*] in the sunlight.

> [*He suddenly sees the huge misshapen bulk of Harlee.*]

O—O—O.

HARLEE—Urh!

THARNI—Why, it's Harlee.

THÁRRABAS—I thought you were some fearful, evil god.

> [*Harlee laughs. He remains leaning on his great iron bar.*]

THARNI—He waits here for the Queen.

THÁRRABAS—What sinister need could she have of Harlee?

THARNI—I know not. You wait for the Queen, Harlee?

> [*Harlee nods.*]

THÁRRABAS—I would not banquet here. Not with a Queen.

> [*Harlee laughs long.*]

Our work is done. Come. Let us leave this place.

> [*Exeunt Thárrabas and Tharni up the steps.*]
> [*The Queen appears with her handmaid, Ackazárpses, coming down the steps. Her handmaid holds her train. They enter the temple.*]

QUEEN—Ah, all is ready.

ACKAZÁRPSES—No, no, Illustrious Lady. Nothing is ready. Your raiment—we must fasten it here [*shoulder*], and then the bow in your hair.

> [*She begins to tittivate the Queen.*]

QUEEN—Ackazárpses, Ackazárpses. I cannot *bear* to have enemies.

ACKAZÁRPSES—Indeed, Illustrious Lady, it is most wrong that you should have enemies. One so delicate, so slender and withal so beautiful should never have a foe.

QUEEN—If the gods could understand they would never permit it.

ACKAZÁRPSES—I have poured out dark wine to them, I have offered them fat, indeed, I have often offered them savoury things. I have said: "The

Queen should not have enemies; she is too delicate, too fair." But they will not understand.

QUEEN–If they could see my tears they would never permit such woes to be borne by one small woman.
But they only look at men and their horrible
wars. Why must men slay one another and make
horrible war?

ACKAZÁRPSES–I blame your enemies, Illustrious Lady,
more than the gods. Why should they trouble
you who are so fair and so easily hurt by their
anger? It was but a little territory you took from
them. How much better to lose a little territory
than to be unmannerly and unkind.

QUEEN–O speak not of the territory. I know naught of
these things. They say my captains took it. How
should I know? O why will they be my enemies?

ACKAZÁRPSES–You are most fair to-night, Illustrious Lady.

QUEEN–I must needs be fair to-night.

ACKAZÁRPSES–Indeed you are most fair.

QUEEN–A little more perfume, Ackazárpses.

ACKAZÁRPSES–I will tie the coloured bow more evenly.

QUEEN–O they will never look at it. They will not know
if it is orange or blue. I shall weep if they do not
look at it. It is a pretty bow.

ACKAZÁRPSES–Calm yourself, lady! They will be here
soon.

QUEEN–Indeed I think they are very close to me now, for
I feel myself trembling.

ACKAZÁRPSES–You must not tremble, Illustrious Lady; you
must not tremble.

QUEEN–They are such terrible men, Ackazárpses.

ACKAZÁRPSES–But you must not tremble, for your raiment
is now perfect; yet if you tremble, alas! who may
say how it will hang?

QUEEN–They are such huge, terrible men.

ACKAZÁRPSES–O the raiment, the raiment; you must not,
you must not!

QUEEN–O I cannot bear it. I cannot bear it. There is
Rhádamandáspes, that huge, fierce soldier, and

the terrible Priest of Horus, and . . . and . . . O
I cannot see them, I cannot see them.

ACKAZÁRPSES–Lady, you have invited them.

QUEEN–O say I am ill, say I am sick of a fever. Quick,
quick, say I have some swift fever and cannot
see them.

ACKAZÁRPSES–Illustrious Lady . . .

QUEEN–Quick, for I cannot bear it.

> *[Exit Ackazárpses.]*

O, I cannot bear to have enemies.

ACKAZÁRPSES *[Returning.]*–Lady, they are here.

QUEEN–O what shall we do? . . . Set this bow higher upon
my head so that it must be seen.

> *[Ackazárpses does so.]*

The pretty bow.

> *[She continues to look in a hand mirror. A
> slave descends the stairs. Then Rhádaman-
> dáspes and Zophérnes. Rhádamandáspes
> and Zophérnes stop; the slave stops lower
> down.]*

ZOPHERNES–For the last time, Rhádamandáspes, consider.
Even yet we may turn back.

RHÁDAMANDÁSPES–She had no guards outside nor was
there any hiding place for them. There was the
empty plain and the Nile only.

ZOPHERNES–Who knows what she may have in this dark
temple?

RHÁDAMANDÁSPES–It is small and the stairway narrow;
our friends are close behind us. We could hold
these steps with our swords against all her men.

ZOPHERNES–True. They are narrow steps. Yet . . . Rhádamandáspes, I do not fear man or god or even
woman, yet when I saw the letter this woman
sent bidding us banquet with her I felt that it
was not well that we should come.

RHÁDAMANDÁSPES–She said that she would love us though
we were her enemies.

ZOPHERNES–It is not natural to love one's enemies.

RHÁDAMANDÁSPES–She is much swayed by whims. They

sway her as the winds in Spring sway flowers—
this way and that. This is one of her whims.

ZOPHERNES—I do not trust her whims.

RHÁDAMANDÁSPES—They name you Zophérnes, giver of
good counsel, therefore I will turn back because
you counsel it, though I would fain go down and
banquet with this little playful lady.

[*They turn and mount.*]

ZOPHERNES—Believe me, Rhádamandáspes, it is better. I
think that if you had gone down these steps we
scarcely should have seen the sky again.

RHÁDAMANDÁSPES—Well, well, we turn back, though I
would fain have humoured the Queen's whim.
But look. The others come. We cannot turn back.
There comes the Priest of Horus; we must go to
the banquet now.

ZOPHERNES—So be it.

[*They descend.*]

RHÁDAMANDÁSPES—We will be circumspect. If she has
men in there we return at once.

ZOPHERNES—So be it.

[*The Slave opens the door.*]

SLAVE—The Princes Rhádamandáspes and Zophérnes.

QUEEN—Welcome, Illustrious Princes.

RHÁDAMANDÁSPES—Greeting.

QUEEN—O you have brought your sword!

RHÁDAMANDÁSPES—I have brought my sword.

QUEEN—O but it is so terrible, your great sword.

ZOPHERNES—We always carry our swords.

QUEEN—O but you do not need them. If you have come to
kill me your great hands are enough. But why
do you bring your swords?

RHÁDAMANDÁSPES—Illustrious Lady, we do not come to
kill you.

QUEEN—To your post, Harlee.

ZOPHERNES—What are this Harlee and his post?

ACKAZÁRPSES—Do not tremble, Illustrious Lady, indeed
you must not tremble.

QUEEN—He is but a fisherman; he lives upon the Nile.

He nets fish; indeed he is nothing.

ZOPHERNES—For what is your great bar of iron, Slave?

> [*Harlee opens his mouth showing that he is tongueless. Exit.*]

RHÁDAMANDÁSPES—Ugh! They have burned out his tongue.

ZOPHERNES—He goes on secret errands.

> [*Enter Second Slave.*]

SECOND SLAVE—The Priest of Horus.

QUEEN—Welcome, holy companion of the gods.

PRIEST OF HORUS—Greeting.

THIRD SLAVE—The King of the Four Countries.

> [*She and he make obeisance.*]

FOURTH SLAVE—The Twin Dukes of Ethiopia.

KING—We are all met.

PRIEST OF HORUS—All that have warred against her captains.

QUEEN—O speak not of my captains. It troubles me to hear of violent men. But you have been my enemies, and I cannot bear to have enemies. Therefore I have asked you to banquet with me.

PRIEST OF HORUS—And we have come.

QUEEN—O look not so sternly at me. I cannot bear to have enemies. When I have enemies I do not sleep. Is it not so, Ackazárpses?

ACKAZÁRPSES—Indeed, the Illustrious Lady has suffered much.

QUEEN—O Ackazárpses, why should I have enemies?

ACKAZÁRPSES—After to-night you will sleep, Illustrious Lady.

QUEEN—Why, yes, for we shall all be friends; shall we not, princes? Let us be seated.

RHÁDAMANDÁSPES [*To Zophérnes.*]—There is no other doorway. That is well.

ZOPHERNES—Why, no, there is not. Yet what is that great hole that is full of darkness?

RHÁDAMANDÁSPES—Only one man at a time could come that way. We are safe from man or beast. Nothing could enter that way for our swords.

QUEEN—I pray you to be seated.

> [*They seat themselves cautiously, she standing watching them.*]

ZOPHERNES—There are no servitors.

QUEEN—Are there not viands before you, Prince Zophérnes, or are there too few fruits that you should blame me?

ZOPHERNES—I do not blame you.

QUEEN—I fear you blame me with your fierce eyes.

ZOPHERNES—I do not blame you.

QUEEN—O my enemies, I would have you kind to me. And indeed there are no servitors, for I know what evil things you think of me . . .

A DUKE OF ETHIOPIA—No, Queen, indeed we think no evil of you.

QUEEN—Ah, but you think terrible things.

PRIEST OF HORUS—We think no evil of you, Illustrious Lady.

QUEEN—I feared that if I had servitors you would think . . . you would say, "This wicked Queen, our enemy, will bid them attack us while we feast."

> [*First Duke of Ethiopia furtively hands food to his Slave standing behind him, who tastes it.*]

Though you do not know how I dread the sight of blood, and indeed I would never bid them do such a thing. The sight of blood is shocking.

PRIEST OF HORUS—We trust you, Illustrious Lady.

> [*He does the same with his Slave.*]

QUEEN—And for miles round this temple and all along the river I have said, "Let there be no man." I have commanded and there are not. Will you not trust me now?

> [*Zophérnes does the same and all the guests, one by one.*]

PRIEST OF HORUS—Indeed, we trust you.

QUEEN—And you, Prince Zophérnes, with your fierce eyes that so frighten me—will you not trust me?

ZOPHERNES—O Queen, it is part of the art of war to be

well prepared when in an enemy's country, and we have been so long at war with your captains that we perforce remember some of the art. It is not that we do not trust you.

QUEEN–I am all alone with my handmaid and none will trust me! O Ackazárpses, I am frightened; what if my enemies should slay me and carry me up, and cast my body into the lonely Nile.

ACKAZÁRPSES–No, no, Illustrious Lady. They will not harm you. They do not know how their fierce looks distress you. They do not know how delicate you are.

PRIEST OF HORUS [*To Ackazárpses.*]–Indeed we trust the Queen and none would harm her.

> [*Ackazárpses soothes the Queen.*]

RHÁDAMANDÁSPES [*To Zophérnes.*]–I think we do wrong to doubt her, seeing she is alone.

ZOPHERNES [*To Rhádamandáspes.*]–Yet I would that the banquet were over.

QUEEN–[*To Ackazárpses and the Priest of Horus, but audible to all.*]

> Yet they do not eat the food that I set before them.

DUKE OF ETHIOPIA–In Ethiopia when we feast with queens it is our custom not to eat at once but to await the Queen till she has eaten.

QUEEN [*Eats.*]–Behold then, I have eaten.

> [*She looks at Priest of Horus.*]

PRIEST OF HORUS–It has been the custom of all that held my office, from the time when there went on earth the children of the Moon, never to eat till the food is dedicated, by our sacred signs, to the gods.

> [*He begins to wave his hands over the food.*]

QUEEN–The King of the Four Countries does not eat. And you, Prince Rhádamandáspes, you have given royal wine unto your slave.

RHÁDAMANDÁSPES–O Queen, it is the custom of our dynasty . . . and has indeed long been so . . . as many say . . . that the noble should not feast till the base have feasted, reminding us that our bodies even as the humble bodies of the base . . .

QUEEN—Why do you thus watch your slave, Prince Rhádamandáspes?

RHÁDAMANDÁSPES—Even to remind myself that I have done as our dynasty doth.

QUEEN—Alas for me, Ackazárpses, they will not feast with me, but mock me because I am little and alone. O I shall not sleep to-night, I shall not sleep.

[*She weeps.*]

ACKAZÁRPSES—Yes, yes, Illustrious Lady, you shall sleep. Be patient and all shall be well and you will sleep.

RHÁDAMANDÁSPES—But Queen, Queen, we are about to eat.

DUKE OF ETHIOPIA—Yes, yes, indeed we do not mock you.

KING OF FOUR COUNTRIES—We do not mock you, Queen.

QUEEN—They . . . give my food to slaves.

PRIEST OF HORUS—That was a mistake.

QUEEN—It was . . . no mistake.

PRIEST OF HORUS—The slaves were hungry.

QUEEN [*Still weeping.*]—They believe I would poison them.

PRIEST OF HORUS—No, no, Illustrious Lady, they do not believe that.

QUEEN—They believe I would poison them.

ACKAZÁRPSES [*Comforting her.*]—O hush, hush. They do not mean to be so cruel.

PRIEST OF HORUS—They do not believe you would poison them. But they do not know if the meat was killed with a poisonous arrow or if an asp may have inadvertently bitten the fruit. These things may happen, but they do not believe you would poison them.

QUEEN—They believe I would poison them.

RHÁDAMANDÁSPES—No; Queen, see, we eat.

[*They hastily whisper to slaves.*]

FIRST DUKE OF ETHIOPIA—We eat your viands, Queen.

SECOND DUKE OF ETHIOPIA—We drink your wine.

KING OF FOUR COUNTRIES—We eat your good pome-
granates and Egyptian grapes.

ZOPHERNES—We eat.

> *[They all eat.]*

PRIEST OF HORUS *[Smiling affably.]*—I *too* eat of your
excellent banquet, O Queen.

> *[He peels a fruit slowly, glancing constantly
> at the others.]*

> *[Meanwhile the catches in the Queen's breath
> grow fewer, she begins to dry her eyes.]*

ACKAZÁRPSES *[In her ear.]*—They eat.

> *[Ackazárpses lifts her head and watches
> them.]*

QUEEN—Perhaps the wine is poisoned.

PRIEST OF HORUS—No, no, Illustrious Lady.

QUEEN—Perhaps the grape was cut by a poisoned arrow.

PRIEST OF HORUS—But indeed . . . indeed . . .

> *[Queen drinks from his cup.]*

QUEEN—Will you not drink my wine?

PRIEST OF HORUS—I drink to our continued friendship.

> *[He drinks.]*

A DUKE OF ETHIOPIA—Our continued friendship!

PRIEST OF HORUS—There has been no true enmity. We mis-
understood the Queen's armies.

RHÁDAMANDÁSPES *[To Zophérnes.]*—We have wronged
the Queen. The wine's not poisoned. Let us drink
to her.

ZOPHERNES—So be it.

RHÁDAMANDÁSPES—We drink to you, Queen.

ZOPHERNES—We drink.

QUEEN—The flagon, Ackazárpses.

> *[Ackazárpses brings it. The Queen pours it
> into her cup.]*

Fill up your goblets from the flagon, princes.

> *[She drinks.]*

RHÁDAMANDÁSPES—We wronged you, Queen. It is a
blessed wine.

QUEEN—It is an ancient wine and grew in Lesbos, looking

from Mytilenë to the South. Ships brought it
over-seas and up this river to gladden the hearts
of man in holy Egypt. But to me it brings no joy.

DUKE OF ETHIOPIA—It is a happy wine, Queen.

QUEEN—I have been thought a poisoner.

PRIEST OF HORUS—Indeed, none has thought that, Illustrious Lady.

QUEEN—You have all thought it.

RHÁDAMANDÁSPES—We ask your pardon, Queen.

KING OF FOUR COUNTRIES—We ask your pardon.

DUKE OF ETHIOPIA—Indeed we erred.

ZOPHERNES [*Rising.*]—We have eaten your fruits and
drunk your wine; and we have asked your
pardon. Let us now depart in amity.

QUEEN—No, no! No, no! You must not go! I shall say . . .
"They are my enemies still," and I shall not
sleep. I that cannot bear to have enemies.

ZOPHERNES—Let us depart in all amity.

QUEEN—O will you not feast with me?

ZOPHERNES—We have feasted.

RHÁDAMANDÁSPES—No, no, Zophérnes. Do you not see?
The Queen takes it to heart.

[*Zophérnes sits down.*]

QUEEN—O feast with me a little longer and make merry,
and be my enemies no more. Rhádamandáspes,
there is some country eastwards towards Assyria,
is there not?—I do not know its name—a country
which your dynasty claims of me . . .

ZOPHERNES—Ha!

RHÁDAMANDÁSPES [*Resignedly.*]—We have lost it.

QUEEN—. . . and for whose sake you are my enemy and
your fierce uncle, Prince Zophérnes.

RHÁDAMANDÁSPES—We fought somewhat with your
armies, Queen. But indeed it was but to practise
the military art.

QUEEN—I will call my captains to me. I will call them
down from their high places and reprove them
and bid them give the country back to you that
lies eastwards towards Assyria. Only you shall

tarry here at the feast and forget you ever were
    my enemies . . . forget . . .

RHÁDAMANDÁSPES–Queen . . . ! Queen . . . ! It was my
    mother's country as a child . . .

QUEEN–You will not leave me alone then here to-night.

RHÁDAMANDÁSPES–No, most royal lady.

QUEEN [*To King of Four Countries who appears about
    to depart.*]–And in the matter of the merchant
    men that trade amongst the isles, they shall offer
    spices at *your* feet, not at mine, and the men of
    the isles shall offer goats to *your* gods.

KING OF FOUR COUNTRIES–Most generous Queen . . .
    indeed . . .

QUEEN–But you will not leave my banquet and go un-
    friendly away.

KING OF FOUR COUNTRIES–No, Queen . . .

[*He drinks.*]

QUEEN [*She looks at the Two Dukes amiably.*]–All
    Ethiopia shall be yours, down to the unknown
    kingdoms of the beasts.

FIRST DUKE OF ETHIOPIA–Queen.

SECOND DUKE OF ETHIOPIA–Queen. We drink to the glory
    of your throne.

QUEEN–Stay then and feast with me. For not to have
    enemies is the beggar's joy; and I have looked
    from windows long and long, envying those that
    go their ways in rags. Stay with me, dukes and
    princes.

PRIEST OF HORUS–Illustrious Lady, the generosity of your
    royal heart has given the gods much joy.

QUEEN [*Smiles at him.*]–Thank you.

PRIEST OF HORUS–Er . . . in the matter of the tribute due
    to Horus from all the people of Egypt . . .

QUEEN–It is yours.

PRIEST OF HORUS–Illustrious Lady.

QUEEN–I will take none of it. Use it how you will.

PRIEST OF HORUS–The gratitude of Horus shall shine on
    you. My little Ackazárpses, how happy you are
    in having so royal a mistress.

[*His arm is round Ackazárpses' waist; Ackazárpses smiles at him.*]

QUEEN [*Rising.*]—Princes and gentlemen, let us drink to
the future.

PRIEST OF HORUS [*Starting suddenly.*]—Ah-h-h!

QUEEN—Something has troubled you, holy companion of
the gods?

PRIEST OF HORUS—No, nothing. Sometimes the spirit of
prophecy comes on me. It comes not often. It
seemed to come then. I thought that one of the
gods spoke to me clearly.

QUEEN—What said he?

PRIEST OF HUROS—I thought he said . . . speaking here
[*right ear*] or just behind me . . . Drink not to
the Future. But it was nothing.

QUEEN—Will you drink then to the past?

PRIEST OF HORUS—O no, Illustrious Lady, for we forget
the past; your good wine has made us forget the
past and its quarrels.

ACKAZÁRPSES—Will you not drink to the present?

PRIEST OF HORUS—Ah, the present! The present that places
me by so lovely a lady. I drink to the present.

QUEEN [*To the others.*] And we, we will drink to the
future, and to forgetting—to the forgetting of
our enemies.

[*All drink; good temper comes on all. The
banquet begins "to go well."*]

QUEEN—Ackazárpses, they are all merry now.

ACHAZÁRPSES—They are all merry.

QUEEN—They are telling Ethiopian tales.

FIRST DUKE OF ETHIOPIA—. . . for when Winter comes the
pigmies at once put themselves in readiness for
war and having chosen a place for battle wait
there for some days, so that the cranes when
they arrive find their enemy already arrayed.
And at first they preen themselves and do not
give battle, but when they are fully rested after
their great journey they attack the pigmies with

indescribable fury so that many are slain, but the pigmies . . .

QUEEN [*Taking her by wrist.*]—Ackazárpses!

[*The Queen rises.*]

ZOPHERNES—Queen, you do not leave us?

QUEEN—For a little while, Prince Zophérnes.

ZOPHERNES—For what purpose?

QUEEN—I go to pray to a very secret god.

ZOPHERNES—What is his name?

QUEEN—His name is secret like his deeds.

[*She goes to door. Silence falls. All watch her. She and Ackazárpses slip out. For a moment silence. Then all draw their wide swords and lay them before them on the table.*]

ZOPHERNES—To the door, slaves. Let no man enter.

FIRST DUKE OF ETHIOPIA—She cannot mean harm to us!

[*A Slave comes back from door and abases himself. Loq.*]

SLAVE—The door is bolted.

RHÁDAMANDÁSPES—It is easily broken with our swords.

ZOPHERNES—No harm can come to us while we guard the entrances.

[*Meanwhile the Queen has gone up the stairs. She beats with a fan on the wall thrice. The great grating lifts outwards and upwards very slowly.*]

ZOPHERNES [*To the Two Dukes.*]—Quick, to the great hole.

[*They go.*]

Stand on each side of it with your swords.

[*They lift their swords over the hole.*]

Slay whatever enters.

QUEEN [*On the step, kneeling, her two arms stretched upwards.*]—O holy Nile! Ancient Egyptian river! O blessed Nile! When I was a little child I played beside you, picking mauve flowers. I threw you down the sweet Egyptian flowers. It is the little Queen that calls to you, Nile. The little Queen that cannot bear to have enemies.

Hear me, O Nile.

Men speak of other rivers. But I do not hearken to fools. There is only Nile. It is the little child that prays to you who used to pick mauve flowers. Hear me, O Nile.

I have prepared a sacrifice to god. Men speak of other gods: there is only Nile. I have prepared a sacrifice of wine—the Lesbian wine from fairy Mytilenë—to mingle with your waters till you are drunken and go singing to the sea from the Abyssinian hills. O Nile, hear me.

Fruits also have I made ready, all the sweet juices of the earth; and the meat of beasts also.

Hear me, O Nile: for it is not the meat of beasts only. I have slaves for you and princes and a King. There has been no such sacrifice.

Come down, O Nile, from the sunlight.

O ancient Egyptian river! The sacrifice is ready.

O Nile, hear me.

DUKE OF ETHIOPIA—No one comes.

QUEEN [*Beats again with her fan.*]—Harlee, Harlee, let in the water upon the princes and gentlemen.

> [*A green torrent descends from the great hole. Green gauzes rise up from the floor; the torches hiss out. The temple is flooded. The water from under the doors rises up the steps; the torches hiss out one by one. The water, finding its own level, just touches the end of the Queen's skirt and stops. She withdraws the skirt with catlike haste from the water.*]

O Ackazárpses! Are all my enemies gone?

ACKAZÁRPSES—Illustrious Lady, the Nile has taken them all.

QUEEN [*With intense devotion.*]—That holy river.

ACKAZÁRPSES—Illustrious Lady, you will sleep to-night?

QUEEN—Yes. I shall sleep sweetly.

CURTAIN

How Plash-Goo
Came to the Land
of None's Desire

In a thatched cottage of enormous size, so vast that we might consider it a palace, but only a cottage in the style of its building, its timbers and the nature of its interior, there lived Plash-Goo.

Plash-Goo was of the children of the giants, whose sire was Uph. And the lineage of Uph had dwindled in bulk for the last five hundred years, till the giants were now no more than fifteen foot high; but Uph ate elephants which he caught with his hands.

Now on the tops of the mountains above the house of Plash-Goo, for Plash-Goo lived in the plains, there dwelt the dwarf whose name was Lrippity-Kang.

And the dwarf used to walk at evening on the edge of the tops of the mountains, and would walk up and down along it, and was squat and ugly and hairy, and was plainly seen of Plash-Goo.

And for many weeks the giant had suffered the sight of him, but at length grew irked at the sight (as men are by little things), and could not sleep of a night and lost his taste for pigs. And at last there came the day, as anyone might have known, when Plash-Goo shouldered his club and went up to look for the dwarf.

And the dwarf though briefly squat was broader than may be dreamed, beyond all breadth of man, and stronger than men may know; strength in its very essence dwelt in that little frame, as a spark in the heart of a flint: but to Plash-Goo he was no more than mis-shapen, bearded and squat, a thing that dared to defy all natural laws by being more broad than long.

When Plash-Goo came to the mountain he cast his chimahalk down (for so he named the club of his heart's desire) lest the dwarf should defy him with nimbleness; and stepped towards Lrippity-Kang with gripping hands, who stopped in his mountainous walk without a word, and swung round his hideous breadth to confront Plash-Goo.

Already then Plash-Goo in the deeps of his mind had seen himself seize the dwarf in one large hand and hurl him with his beard and his hated breadth sheer down the precipice that dropped away from that very place to the land of None's Desire. Yet it was otherwise that Fate would have it. For the dwarf parried with his little arms the grip of those monstrous hands, and gradually working along the enormous limbs came at length to the giant's body where by dwarfish cunning he obtained a grip; and turning Plash-Goo about, as a spider does some great fly, till his little grip was suitable to his purpose, he suddenly lifted the giant over his head. Slowly at first, by the edge of that precipice whose base sheer distance hid, he swung his giant victim round his head, but soon faster and faster; and at last when Plash-Goo was streaming round the hated breadth of the dwarf and the no less hated beard was flapping in the wind, Lrippity-Kang let go. Plash-Goo shot over the edge and for some way further out towards Space, like a stone; then he began to fall. It was long before he believed and truly knew that this was really he that fell from this mountain, for we do not associate such dooms with ourselves; but when he had fallen from some while through the evening and saw below him, where there had been nothing to see, or *began* to see, the glimmer of tiny fields, then his optimism departed; till later on when the fields were greener and larger he saw that this was indeed (and growing now terribly nearer) that very land to which he had destined the dwarf.

At last he saw it unmistakable, close, with its grim houses and its dreadful ways, and its green fields shining in the light of the evening. His cloak was streaming from him in whistling shreds.

So Plash-Goo came to the Land of None's Desire.

The Prayer
of Boob Aheera

In the harbour, between the liner and the palms, as the huge ship's passengers came up from dinner, at moonrise, each in his canoe, Ali Kareeb Ahash and Boob Aheera passed within knife thrust.

So urgent was the purpose of Ali Kareeb Ahash that he did not lean over as his enemy slid by, did not tarry then to settle that long account; but that Boob Aheera made no attempt to reach him was a source of wonder to Ali. He pondered it till the liner's electric lights shone far away behind him with one blaze and the canoe was near to his destination, and pondered it in vain, for all that the eastern sublety of his mind was able to tell him clearly was that it was not like Boob Aheera to pass him by like that.

That Boob Aheera could have dared to lay such a cause as his before the Diamond Idol Ali had not conceived, yet as he drew near to the golden shrine in the palms, that none that come by the great ships ever found, he began to see more clearly in his mind that this was where Boob had gone on that hot night. And when he beached his canoe his fears departed, giving place to the resignation with which he always viewed Destiny; for there on the white sea sand were the tracks of another canoe, the edges all fresh and ragged. Boob Aheera had been before him. Ali did not blame himself for being late, the thing had been planned before the beginning of time, by gods that knew their business; only his hate of Boob Aheera increased, his enemy against whom he had come to pray. And the more his hate increased the more clearly he saw him, until nothing else could be seen by the eye of his mind but the dark lean figure, the little lean legs, the grey beard and neat loin-cloth of Boob Aheera, his enemy.

That the Diamond Idol should have granted the prayers of such a one he did not as yet imagine, he hated him merely for his presumptuousness in approaching the shrine at all, for approaching it before him whose cause was righteous, for many an old past wrong, but most of all for the expression of his face and the general look of the man as he had swept by in his canoe with his double paddle going in the moonlight.

Ali pushed through the steaming vegetation. The place smelt of orchids. There is no track to the shrine though many go. If there were a track the white man would one day find it, and parties would row to see it whenever a liner came in; and photographs would appear in weekly papers with accounts of it underneath by men who had never left London, and all the mystery would be gone away and there would be nothing novel in this story.

Ali had scarcely gone a hundred yards through cactus and creeper underneath the palms when he came to the golden shrine that nothing guards except the deeps of the forest, and found the Diamond Idol. The Diamond Idol is five inches high and its base a good inch square, and it has greater lustre than those diamonds that Mr. Moses bought last year for his wife, when he offered her an earldom or the diamonds, and Jael his wife had answered: "Buy the diamonds and be just plain Mr. Fortescue."

Purer than those was its lustre and carved as they carve not in Europe, and the men thereby are poor and held to be fearless—yet they do not sell that idol. And I may say here that if any one of my readers should ever come by ship to the winding harbour where the forts of the Portuguese crumble in infinite greenery, where the baobab stands like a corpse here and there in the palms, if he goes ashore where no one has any business to go, and where no one so far as

I know has gone from a liner before (though it's little more than a mile or so from the pier), and if he finds a golden shrine, which is near enough to the shore, and a five-inch diamond in it carved in the shape of a god, it is better to leave it alone and get back safe to the ship than to sell that diamond idol for any price in the world.

Ali Kareeb Ahash went into the golden shrine, and when he raised his head from the seven obeisances that are the due of the idol, behold! it glowed with such a lustre as only it wears after answering recent prayer. No native of those parts mistakes the tone of the idol, they know its varying shades as a tracker knows blood; the moon was streaming in through the open door and Ali saw it clearly.

No one had been that night but Boob Aheera.

The fury of Ali rose and surged to his heart, he clutched his knife till the hilt of it bruised his hand, yet he did not utter the prayer that he had made ready about Boob Aheera's liver, for he saw that Boob Aheera's prayers were acceptable to the idol and knew that divine protection was over his enemy.

What Boob Aheera's prayer was he did not know, but he went back to the beach as fast as one can go through cacti and creepers that climb to the tops of the palms; and as fast as his canoe could carry him he went down the winding harbour, till the liner shone beside him as he passed, and he heard the sound of its band rise up and die, and he landed and came that night into Boob Aheera's hut. And there he offered himself as his enemy's slave, and Boob Aheera's slave he is to this day, and his master has protection from the idol. And Ali rows to the liners and goes on board to sell rubies made of glass, and thin suits for the tropics and ivory napkin rings, and Manchester kimonos, and little lovely shells; and the passengers abuse him because of his prices; and yet they should not, for all the money cheated by Ali Kareeb Ahash goes to Boob Aheera, his master.

East and West

It was dead of night and midwinter. A frightful wind was bringing sleet from the East. The long sere grasses were wailing. Two specks of light appeared on the desolate plain; a man in a hansom cab was driving alone in North China.

Alone with the driver and the dejected horse. The driver wore a good waterproof cape, and of course an oiled silk hat, but the man in the cab wore nothing but evening dress. He did not have the glass door down because the horse fell so frequently, the sleet had put his cigar out and it was too cold to sleep; the two lamps flared in the wind. By the uncertain light of a candle lamp that flickered inside the cab, a Manchu shepherd that saw the vehicle pass, where he watched his sheep on the plain in fear of the wolves, for the first time saw evening dress. And though he saw it dimly, and what he saw was wet, it was like a backward glance of a thousand years, for as his civilization is so much older than ours they have presumably passed through all that kind of thing.

He watched it stoically, not wondering at a new thing, if indeed it be new to China, meditated on it awhile in a manner strange to us, and when he had added to his philosophy what little could be derived from the sight of this hansom cab, returned to his contemplation of that night's chances of wolves and to such occasional thoughts as he drew at times for his comfort out of the legends of China, that have been preserved for such uses. And on such a night their comfort was greatly needed. He thought of the legend of a dragon-lady, more fair than the flowers are, without an equal amongst daughters of men, humanly lovely to look on although her sire was a dragon, yet one who traced his descent from gods of the elders days, and so it was that she went in all her ways divine, like the earliest ones of her race, who were holier than the emperor.

She had come down one day out of her little land, a grassy valley hidden amongst the mountains; by the way of the mountain passes she came down, and the rocks of the rugged pass rang like little bells about her, as her bare feet went by, like silver bells to please her; and the sound was like the sound of the dromedaries of a prince when they come home at evening—their silver bells are ringing and the village-folk are glad. She had come down to pick the enchanted poppy that grew, and grows to this day—if only men might find it—in a field at the feet of the mountains; if one should pick it happiness would come to all yellow men, victory without fighting, good wages, and ceaseless ease. She came down all fair from the mountains; and as the legend pleasantly passed through his mind in the bitterest hour of the night, which comes before dawn, two lights appeared and another hansom went by.

The man in the second cab was dressed the same as the first, he was wetter than the first, for the sleet had fallen all night, but evening dress is evening dress all the world over. The driver wore the same oiled hat, the same waterproof cape as the other. And when the cab had passed the darkness swirled back where the two small lamps had been, and the slush poured into the wheel-tracks and nothing remained but the speculations of the shepherd to tell that a hansom cab had been in that part of China; presently even these ceased, and he was back with the the early legends again in contemplation of serener things.

And the storm and the cold and the darkness made one last effort, and shook the bones of that shepherd, and rattled the teeth in the head that mused on the flowery fables, and suddenly it was morning. You saw the outlines of the sheep all of a sudden, the shepherd counted them, no wolf had come, you could see them all quite clearly. And in the pale light of the earliest morning the third hansom appeared, with its lamps still burning, looking ridiculous in the daylight. They came out of the East with the sleet and were all going due westwards, and the occupant of the third cab also wore evening dress.

Calmly that Manchu shepherd, without curiosity, still less with wonder, but as one who would see whatever life has to show him, stood for four hours to see if another would come. The sleet and the East wind continued. And at the end of four hours another came. The driver was urging it on as fast as he could, as though he were trying to make the most of the daylight, his cabby's cape was flapping wildly about him; inside the cab a man in evening dress was being jolted up and down by the unevenness of the plain.

This was of course that famous race from Pittsburg to Piccadilly, going round by the long way, that started one night after dinner from Mr. Flagdrop's house, and was won by Mr. Kagg, driving the Honourable Alfred Fortescue, whose father it will be remembered was Hagar Dermstein, and became (by Letters Patent) Sir Edgar Fortescue, and finally Lord St. George.

The Manchu shepherd stood there till evening, and when he saw that no more cabs would come, turned homeward in search of food.

And the rice prepared for him was hot and good, all the more after the bitter coldness of that sleet. And when he had consumed it he perused his experience, turning over again in his mind each detail of the cabs he had seen; and from that his thoughts slipped calmly to the glorious history of China, going back to the indecorous times before calmness came, and beyond those times to the happy days of the earth when the gods and dragons were here and China was young; and lighting his opium pipe and casting his thoughts easily forward he looked to the time when the dragons shall come again.

And for a long while then his mind reposed itself in such a dignified calm that no thought stirred there at all, from which when he was aroused he cast off his lethargy as a man emerges from the baths, refreshed, cleansed and contented, and put away from his musings the things he had seen on the plain as being evil and of the nature of dreams, or futile illusion, the results of activity which troubleth calm. And then he turned his mind toward the shape of God, the One, the Ineffable, who sits by the lotus lily, whose shape is the shape of peace, and denieth activity, and sent out his thanks to him that he had cast all bad customs westward out of China as a woman throws household dirt out of her basket far out into neighbouring gardens.

From thankfulness he turned to calm again, and out of calm to sleep.

How the Gods
Avenged
Meoul Ki Ning

Meoul Ki Ning was on his way with a lily from the lotus
ponds of Esh to offer it to the Goddess of Abundance
in her temple Aoul Keroon. And on the road from the
pond to the little hill and the temple Aoul Keroon, Ap
Ariph, his enemy, shot him with an arrow from a bow
that he had made out of bamboo, and took his pretty
lily up the hill and offered it to the Goddess of Abundance in her temple Aoul Keroon. And the Goddess
was pleased with the gift, as all women are, and sent
pleasant dreams to Ap Ariph for seven nights straight
from the moon.

And on the seventh night the gods held conclave
together, on the cloudy peaks they held it, above
Narn, Ktoon and Pti. So high their peak arises that no
man heard their voices. They spake on that cloudy
mountain (not the highest hamlet heard them). "What
doth the Goddess of Abundance," (but naming her
Lling, as they name her), "what doth she sending sweet
dreams for seven nights to Ap Ariph?"

And the gods sent for their seer who is all eyes
and feet, running to and fro on the Earth, observing the
ways of men, seeing even their littlest doings, never
deeming a doing too little, but knowing the web of
the gods is woven of littlest things. He it is that sees
the cat in the garden of parrakeets, the thief in the
upper chamber, the sin of the child with the honey,
the women talking indoors and the small hut's inner-
most things. Standing before the gods he told them the
case of Ap Ariph and the wrongs of Meoul Ki Ning
and the rape of the lotus lily; he told of the cutting
and making of Ap Ariph's bamboo bow, of the shooting

of Meoul Ki Ning, and of how the arrow hit him, and the smile on the face of Lling when she came by the lotus bloom.

And the gods were wroth with Ap Ariph and swore to avenge Ki Ning.

And the ancient one of the gods, he that is older than Earth, called up the thunder at once, and raised his arms and cried out on the gods' high windy mountain, and prophesied on those rocks with runes that were older than speech, and sang in his wrath old songs that he learned in storm from the sea, when only that peak of the gods in the whole of the earth was dry; and he swore that Ap Ariph should die that night, and the thunder raged about him, and the tears of Lling were vain.

The lightning stroke of the gods leaping earthward seeking Ap Ariph passed near to his house but missed him. A certain vagabond was down from the hills, singing songs in the street near by the house of Ap Ariph, songs of a former folk that dwelt once, they say, in those valleys, and begging for rice and curds; it was him the lightning hit.

And the gods were satisfied, and their wrath abated, and their thunder rolled away and the great black clouds dissolved, and the ancient one of the gods went back to his age-old sleep, and morning came, and the birds and the light shone on the mountain, and the peak stood clear to see, the serene home of the gods.

The Man with the Golden
Ear-rings

It may be that I dreamed this. So much at least is certain—that I turned one day from the traffic of a city, and came to its docks and saw its slimy wharves going down green and steep into the water, and saw the huge grey river slipping by and the lost things that went with it turning over and over, and I thought of the nations and unpitying Time, and saw and marvelled at the queenly ships come newly from the sea.

It was then, if I mistake not, that I saw leaning against a wall, with his face to the ships, a man with golden ear-rings. His skin had the dark tint of the southern men: the deep black hairs of his moustache were whitened a little with salt; he wore a dark blue jacket such as sailors wear, and the long boots of seafarers, but the look in his eyes was further afield than the ships, he seemed to be beholding the farthest things.

Even when I spoke to him he did not call home that look, but answered me dreamily with that same fixed stare as though his thoughts were heaving on far and lonely seas. I asked him what ship he had come by, for there were many there. The sailing ships were there with their sails all furled and their masts straight and still like a wintry forest; the steamers were there, and great liners, puffing up idle smoke into the twilight. He answered he had come by none of them. I asked him what line he worked on, for he was clearly a sailor; I mentioned well-known lines, but he did not know them. Then I asked him where he worked and what he was. And he said: "I work in the Sargasso Sea, and I am the last of the pirates, the last left alive." And I shook him by the hand I do not know how many times. I said: "We feared you were dead. We feared you were dead." And he answered sadly: "No. No. I have sinned too deeply on the Spanish seas: I am not allowed to die."

Poor Old Bill

On an antique haunt of sailors, a tavern of the sea, the light of day was fading. For several evenings I had frequented this place, in the hope of hearing something from the sailors, as they sat over strange wines, about a rumor that had reached my ears of a certain fleet of galleons of old Spain still said to be afloat in the South Seas in some uncharted region.

In this I was again to be disappointed. Talk was low and seldom, and I was about to leave, when a sailor, wearing ear-rings of pure gold, lifted up his head from his wine, and looking straight before him at the wall, told his tale loudly:

(When later on a storm of rain arose and thundered on the tavern's leaded panes, he raised his voice without effort and spoke on still. The darker it got the clearer his wild eyes shone.)

"A ship with sails of the olden time was nearing fantastic isles. We had never seen such isles.

"We all hated the captain, and he hated us. He hated us all alike, there was no favouritism about him. And he never would talk a word with any of us, except sometimes in the evening when it was getting dark he would stop and look up and talk a bit to the men he had hanged at the yard-arm.

"We were a mutinous crew. But Captain was the only man that had pistols. He slept with one under his pillow and kept one close beside him. There was a nasty look about the isles. They were small and flat as though they had come up only recently from the sea, and they had no sand or rocks like honest isles, but green grass down to the water. And there were little cottages there whose looks we did not like. Their thatches came almost down to the ground, and were strangely turned up at the corners, and under the low eaves were queer dark windows whose little leaded panes were too thick to see through. And no one, man or beast, was walking about, so that you could not know what kind of people lived there. But Captain knew. And he went ashore and into one of the cottages, and someone lit lights inside, and the little windows wore an evil look.

"It was quite dark when he came aboard again, and he bade a cheery good-night to the men that swung from the yard-arm, and he eyed us in a way that frightened poor old Bill.

"Next night we found that he had learned to curse, for he came on a lot of us asleep in our bunks, and among them poor old Bill, and he pointed at us with a finger, and made a curse that our souls should stay all night at the top of the masts. And suddenly there was the soul of poor old Bill sitting like a monkey at the top of the mast, and looking at the stars, and freezing through and through.

"We got up a little mutiny after that, but Captain comes up and points with his finger again, and this time poor old Bill and all the rest are swimming behind the ship through the cold green water, though their bodies remain on deck.

"It was the cabin-boy who found out that Captain couldn't curse when he was drunk, though he could shoot as well at one time as another.

"After that it was only a matter of waiting, and of losing two men when the time came. Some of us were murderous fellows, and wanted to kill Captain, but poor old Bill was for finding a bit of an island, out of the track of ships, and leaving him there with his share of our year's provisions. And everybody listened to poor old Bill, and we decided to maroon Captain as soon as we caught him when he couldn't curse.

"It was three whole days before Captain got drunk

again, and poor old Bill and all had a dreadful time, for Captain invented new curses every day, and wherever he pointed his finger our souls had to go; and the fishes got to know us, and so did the stars, and none of them pitied us when we froze on the masts or were hurried through forests of seaweed and lost our way—both stars and fishes went about their businesses with cold, unastonished eyes. Once when the sun had set and it was twilight, and the moon was showing clearer and clearer in the sky, and we stopped our work for a moment because Captain seemed to be looking away from us at the colours in the sky, he suddenly turned and sent our souls to the Moon. And it was colder there than ice at night; and there were horrible mountains making shadows; and it was all as silent as miles of tombs; and Earth was shining up in the sky as big as the blade of a scythe, and we all got homesick for it, but could not speak nor cry. It was quite dark when we got back, and we were very respectful to Captain all the next day, but he cursed several of us again very soon. What we all feared most was that he would curse our souls to Hell, and none of us mentioned Hell above a whisper for fear that it should remind him. But on the third evening the cabin-boy came and told us that the Captain was drunk. And we all went to his cabin, and we found him lying there across his bunk, and he shot as he had never shot before; but he had no more than the two pistols, and he would only have killed two men if he hadn't caught Joe over the head with the end of one of his pistols. And then we tied him up. And poor old Bill put the rum between Captain's teeth, and kept him drunk for two days, so that he could not curse, till we found a convenient rock. And before sunset of the second day we found a nice bare island for Captain, out of the track of ships, about a hundred yards long and about eighty wide; and we rowed him along to it in a little boat, and gave him provisions for a year, the same as we had ourselves, because poor old Bill wanted to be fair. And we left him sitting comfortable with his back to a rock singing a sailor's song.

"When we could no longer hear Captain singing we all grew very cheerful and made a banquet out of our year's provisions, as we all hoped to be home again in under three weeks. We had three great banquets every day for a week—every man had more than he could eat, and what was left over we threw on the floor like gentlemen. And then one day, as we saw San Huëlgédos, and wanted to sail in to spend our money, the wind changed round from behind us and beat us out to sea. There was no tacking against it, and no getting into the harbor, though other ships sailed by us and anchored there. Sometimes a dead calm would fall on us, while fishing boats all around us flew before half a gale, and sometimes the wind would beat us out to sea when nothing else was moving. All day we tried, and at night we laid to and tried again next day. And all the sailors of the other ships were spending their money in San Huëlgédos and we could not come nigh it. Then we spoke horrible things against the wind and against San Huëlgédos, and sailed away.

"It was just the same at Norenna.

"We kept close together now and talked in low voices. Suddenly poor old Bill grew frightened. As we went all along the Siractic coast-line, we tried again and again, and the wind was waiting for us in every harbour and sent us out to sea. Even the little islands would not have us. And then we knew that there was no landing yet for poor old Bill, and every one upbraided his kind heart that had made them maroon Captain on a rock, so as not to have his blood upon their heads. There was nothing to do but to drift about the seas. There were no banquets now, because we feared that Captain might live his year and keep us out to sea.

"At first we used to hail all passing ships, and used to try to board them in the boats; but there was no rowing against Captain's curse, and we had to give that up. So we played cards for a year in Captain's cabin, night and day, storm and fine, and every one promised to pay poor old Bill when we got ashore.

"It was horrible to us to think what a frugal man Captain really was, he that used to get drunk every other day whenever he was at sea, and here he was still alive, and sober too, for his curse still kept us out of every port, and our provisions were gone.

"Well, it came to drawing lots, and Jim was the unlucky one. Jim only kept us about three days, and then we drew lots again, and this time it was the nigger. The nigger didn't keep us any longer, and we drew again, and this time it was Charlie, and still Captain was alive.

"As we got fewer one of us kept us longer. Longer and longer a mate used to last us, and we all wondered how ever Captain did it. It was five weeks over the year when we drew Mike, and he kept us for a week, and Captain was still alive. We wondered he didn't get tired of the same old curse; but we supposed things looked different when one is alone on an island.

"When there was only Jakes and poor old Bill and the cabin-boy and Dick, we didn't draw any longer. We said that the cabin-boy had had all the luck, and he mustn't expect any more. Then poor old Bill was alone with Jakes and Dick, and Captain was still alive. When there was no more boy, and the Captain still alive, Dick, who was a huge strong man like poor old Bill, said that it was Jakes' turn, and he was very lucky to have lived as long as he had. But poor old Bill talked it all over with Jakes, and they thought it better that Dick should take his turn.

"Then there was Jakes and poor old Bill; and Captain would not die.

"And these two used to watch one another night and day, when Dick was gone and no one else was left to them. And at last poor old Bill fell down in a faint and lay there for an hour. Then Jakes came up to him slowly with his knife, and makes a stab at poor old

Bill as he lies there on the deck. And poor old Bill caught hold of him by the wrist, and put his knife into him twice to make quite sure, although it spoiled the best part of the meat. Then poor old Bill was all alone at sea.

"And the very next week, before the food gave out, Captain must have died on his bit of an island; for poor old Bill heard Captain's soul going cursing over the sea, and the day after that the ship was cast on a rocky coast.

"And Captain's been dead now for over a hundred years, and poor old Bill is safe ashore again. But it looks as if Captain hadn't done with him yet, for poor old Bill doesn't ever get any older, and somehow or other he doesn't seem to die. Poor old Bill!"

When this was over the man's fascination suddenly snapped, and we all jumped up and left him.

It was not only his revolting story, but it was the fearful look in the eyes of the man who told it, and the terrible ease with which his voice surpassed the roar of the rain, that decided me never again to enter that haunt of sailors—the tavern of the sea.

Tales of
Near at Hand

Editor's Note

LORD DUNSANY also wrote some stories laid in surroundings which are neither foreign nor alien—such as those which follow next.

I include them here for the very good reason that they display an aspect of his genius we might otherwise easily overlook, blinded to it by the exotic color and glamor of such tales as "The House of the Sphinx" and "Bwona Khubla." For it does take a sensibility of the rarest sort to find romance and mystery in the familiar settings of the Waking World. And in such stories as "The Little City"—and, most particularly, "The Field"—that facet of his talent is brilliantly manifested.

L.C.

The Bad Old Woman in Black

The bad old woman in black ran down the street of the ox-butchers.

Windows at once were opened high up in those crazy gables; heads were thrust out: it was she. Then there arose the counsel of anxious voices, calling sideways from window to window or across to opposite houses. Why was she there with her sequins and bugles and old black gown? Why had she left her dreaded house? On what fell errand she hasted?

They watched her lean, lithe figure, and the wind in that old black dress, and soon she was gone from the cobbled street and under the town's high gateway. She turned at once to her right and was hid from the view of the houses. Then they all ran down to their doors, and small groups formed on the pavement; there they took counsel together, the eldest speaking first. Of what they had seen they said nothing, for there was no doubt it was she; it was of the future they spoke, and the future only.

In what notorious thing would her errand end? What gains had tempted her out from her fearful home? What brilliant but sinful scheme had her genius planned? Above all, what future evil did this portend? Thus at first it was only questions. And then the old grey-beards spoke, each one to a little group; they had seen her out before, had known her when she was younger, and had noted the evil things that had followed her goings: the small groups listened well to their low and earnest voices. No one asked questions now or guessed at her infamous errand, but listened only to the wise old men who knew the things that had been, and who told the younger men of the dooms that had come before.

Nobody knew how many times she had left her dreaded house; but the oldest recounted all the times that they knew, and the way she had gone each time, and the doom that had followed her going; and two could remember the earthquake that there was in the street of the shearers.

So were there many tales of the times that were, told on the pavement near the old green doors by the edge of the cobbled street, and the experience that the aged men had bought with their white hairs might be had cheap by the young. But from all their experience only this was clear, that never twice in their lives had she done the same infamous thing, and that the same calamity twice had never followed her goings. Therefore it seemed that means were doubtful and few for finding out what thing was about to befall; and an ominous feeling of gloom came down on the street of the ox-butchers. And in the gloom grew fears of the very worst. This comfort they only had when they put their fear into words—that the doom that followed her goings had never yet been anticipated. One feared that with magic she meant to move the moon; and he would have dammed the high tide on the neighbouring coast, knowing that as the moon attracted the sea the sea must attract the moon, and hoping by his device to humble her spells. Another would have fetched iron bars and clamped them across the street, remembering the earthquake there was in the street of the shearers. Another would have honoured his household gods, the little cat-faced idols seated above his hearth, gods to whom magic was no unusual thing, and, having paid their fees and honoured them well, would have put the whole case before them. His scheme found favour with many, and yet at last was rejected, for others ran indoors and brought out their gods too, to be honoured, till there was a herd of gods all seated there on the pavement; yet would they have honoured them and put their case before them but that a fat man ran up last of all, carefully holding under a reverent arm his own two hound-faced gods, though he knew well—as, indeed, all men must—that they were notoriously at war with the little cat-faced idols. And although the animosities natural to faith had all been lulled by the crisis, yet a look of anger had come in the cat-like faces that no one dared disregard, and all perceived that if they stayed a moment longer there would be flaming around them the jealousy of the gods; so each man hastily took his idols home, leaving the fat man insisting that his hound-faced gods should be honoured.

Then were there schemes again and voices raised in debate, and many new dangers feared and new plans made.

But in the end they made no defence against danger, for they knew not what it would be, but wrote upon parchment as a warning and in order that all might know: *"The bad old woman in black ran down the street of the ox-butchers."*

The Field

When one has seen Spring's blossom fall in London, and
Summer appear and ripen and decay, as it does early in
cities, and one is in London still, then, at some moment
or another, the country places lift their flowery heads
and call to one with an urgent, masterful clearness upland behind upland in the twilight like to some heavenly
choir arising rank on rank to call a drunkard from his
gambling-hell. No volume of traffic can drown the
sound of it, no lure of London can weaken its appeal.
Having heard it one's fancy is gone, and evermore
departed, to some coloured pebble a-gleam in a rural
brook, and all that London can offer is swept from one's
mind like some suddenly smitten metropolitan Goliath.

The call is from afar both in leagues and years, for
the hills that call one are the hills that were, and
their voices are the voices of long ago, when the elf-
kings still had horns.

I see them now, those hills of my infancy (for it is
they that call), with their faces upturned to the purple
twilight, and the faint diaphanous figures of the fairies
peering out from under the bracken to see if evening
is come. I do not see upon their regal summits those
desirable mansions, and highly desirable residences,
which have lately been built for gentlemen who would
exchange customers for tenants.

When the hills called I used to go to them by road,
riding a bicycle. If you go by train you miss the gradual
approach, you do not cast off London like an old for-
given sin, nor pass by little villages on the way that
must have some rumour of the hills; nor, wondering if
they are still the same, come at last upon the edge of

their far-spread robes, and so on to their feet, and see far off their holy, welcoming faces. In the train you see them suddenly round a curve, and there they all are sitting in the sun.

I imagine that as one penetrated out from some enormous forest of the tropics, the wild beasts would become fewer, the gloom would lighten, and the horror of the place would slowly lift. Yet as one emerges nearer to the edge of London, and nearer to the beautiful influence of the hills, the houses become uglier, the streets viler, the gloom deepens, the errors of civilisation stand bare to the scorn of the fields.

Where ugliness reaches the height of its luxuriance, in the dense misery of the place, where one imagines the builder saying, "Here I culminate. Let us give thanks to Satan," there is a bridge of yellow brick, and through it, as through some gate of filigree silver opening on fairyland, one passes into the country.

To left and right, as far as one can see, stretches that monstrous city; before one are the fields like an old, old song.

There is a field there that is full of king-cups. A stream runs through it, and along the stream is a little wood of oziers. There I used often to rest at the stream's edge before my long journey to the hills.

There I used to forget London, street by street. Sometimes I picked a bunch of king-cups to show them to the hills.

I often came there. At first I noticed nothing about the field except its beauty and its peacefulness.

But the second time that I came I thought there was something ominous about the field.

Down there among the king-cups by the little shallow stream I felt that something terrible might happen in just such a place.

I did not stay long there, because I thought that too much time spent in London had brought on these morbid fancies and I went on to the hills as fast as I could.

I stayed for some days in the country air, and when I came back I went to the field again to enjoy that peaceful spot before entering London. But there was still something ominous among the oziers.

A year elapsed before I went there again. I emerged from the shadow of London into the gleaming sun, the bright green grass and the king-cups were flaming in the light, and the little stream was singing a happy song. But the moment I stepped into the field my old uneasiness returned, and worse than before. It was as though the shadow was brooding there of some dreadful future thing, and a year had brought it nearer.

I reasoned that the exertion of bicycling might be bad for one, and that the moment one rested this uneasiness might result.

A little later I came back past the field by night, and the song of the stream in the hush attracted me down to it. And there the fancy came to me that it would be a terribly cold place to be in in the starlight, if for some reason one was hurt and could not get away.

I knew a man who was minutely acquainted with the past history of that locality, and him I asked if anything historical had ever happened in that field. When he pressed me for my reason in asking him this, I said that the field had seemed to me such a good place to hold a pageant in. But he said that nothing of any interest had ever occurred there, nothing at all.

So it was from the future that the field's trouble came.

For three years off and on I made visits to the field, and every time more clearly it boded evil things, and my uneasiness grew more acute every time that I was lured to go and rest among the cool green grass under the beautiful oziers. Once to distract my thoughts I tried to gauge how fast the stream was trickling, but I found myself wondering if it flowed faster than blood.

I felt that it would be a terrible place to go mad in, one would hear voices.

At last I went to a poet whom I knew, and woke

him from huge dreams, and put before him the whole
case of the field. He had not been out of London all
that year, and he promised to come with me and look
at the field, and tell me what was going to happen there.
It was late in July when we went. The pavement, the
air, the houses and the dirt had been all baked dry
by the summer, the weary traffic dragged on, and on,
and on, and Sleep spreading her wings soared up and
floated from London and went to walk beautifully in
rural places.

When the poet saw the field he was delighted, the
flowers were out in masses all along the stream, he went
down to the little wood rejoicing. By the side of the
stream he stood and seemed very sad. Once or twice
he looked up and down it mournfully, then he bent
and looked at the king-cups, first one and then another, very closely, and shaking his head.

For a long while he stood in silence, and all my
old uneasiness returned, and my bodings for the future.

And then I said "What manner of field is it?"

And he shook his head sorrowfully.

"It is a battlefield," he said.

Where the Tides
Ebb and Flow

I dreamt that I had done a horrible thing, so that burial was to be denied me either in soil or sea, neither could there be any hell for me.

I waited for some hours, knowing this. Then my friends came for me, and slew me secretly and with ancient rite, and lit great tapers, and carried me away.

It was all in London that the thing was done, and they went furtively at dead of night along grey streets and among mean houses until they came to the river. And the river and the tide of the sea were grappling with one another between the mud-banks, and both of them were black and full of lights. A sudden wonder came into the eyes of each, as my friends came near to them with their glaring tapers. All these things I saw as they carried me dead and stiffening, for my soul was still among my bones, because there was no hell for it, and because Christian burial was denied me.

They took me down a stairway that was green with slimy things, and so came slowly to the terrible mud. There, in the territory of forsaken things, they dug a shallow grave. When they had finished they laid me in the grave, and suddenly they cast their tapers to the river. And when the water had quenched the flaring lights the tapers looked pale and small as they bobbed upon the tide, and at once the glamour of the calamity was gone, and I noticed then the approach of the huge dawn; and my friends cast their cloaks over their faces, and the solemn procession was turned into many fugitives that furtively stole away.

Then the mud came back wearily and covered all

but my face. There I lay alone with quite forgotten things, with drifting things that the tides will take no farther, with useless things and lost things, and with the horrible unnatural bricks that are neither stone nor soil. I was rid of feeling, because I had been killed, but perception and thought were in my unhappy soul. The dawn widened, and I saw the desolate houses that crowded the marge of the river, and their dead windows peered into my dead eyes, windows with bales behind them instead of human souls. I grew so weary looking at these forlorn things that I wanted to cry out, but could not because I was dead. Then I knew, as I had never known before, that for all the years that herd of desolate houses had wanted to cry out too, but, being dead, were dumb. And I knew then that it had yet been well with the forgotten drifting things if they had wept, but they were eyeless and without life. And I, too, tried to weep, but there were no tears in my dead eyes. And I knew then that the river might have cared for us, might have caressed us, might have sung to us, but he swept broadly onwards, thinking of nothing but the princely ships.

At last the tide did what the river would not, and came and covered me over, and my soul had rest in the green water, and rejoiced and believed that it had the Burial of the Sea. But with the ebb the water fell again, and left me alone again with the callous mud among the forgotten things that drift no more, and with the sight of all those desolate houses, and with the knowledge among all of us that each was dead.

In the mournful wall behind me, hung with green weeds, forsaken of the sea, dark tunnels appeared, and secret narrow passages that were clamped and barred. From these at last the stealthy rats came down to nibble me away, and my soul rejoiced thereat and believed that he would be free perforce from the accursed bones to which burial was refused. Very soon the rats ran away a little space and whispered among themselves. They never came any more. When I found that I was accursed even among the rats I tried to weep again.

Then the tide came swinging back and covered the dreadful mud, and hid the desolate houses, and soothed the forgotten things, and my soul had ease for a while in the sepulture of the sea. And then the tide forsook me again.

To and fro it came about me for many years. Then the County Council found me, and gave me decent burial. It was the first grave that I had ever slept in. That very night my friends came for me. They dug me up and put me back again in the shallow hole in the mud.

Again and again through the years my bones found burial, but always behind the funeral lurked one of those terrible men who as soon as night fell, came and dug them up and carried them back again to the hole in the mud.

And then one day the last of those men died who once had done to me this terrible thing. I heard his soul go over the river at sunset.

And again I hoped.

A few weeks afterwards I was found once more, and once more taken out of that restless place and given deep burial in sacred ground, where my soul hoped that it should rest.

Almost at once men came with cloaks and tapers to give me back to the mud, for the thing had become a tradition and a rite. And all the forsaken things mocked me in their dumb hearts when they saw me carried back, for they were jealous of me because I had left the mud. It must be remembered that I could not weep.

And the years went by seawards where the black barges go, and the great derelict centuries became lost at sea, and still I lay there without any cause to hope, and daring not to hope without a cause, because of the terrible envy and the anger of the things that could drift no more.

Once a great storm rode up, even as far as London, out of the sea from the South; and he came curving into the river with the fierce East wind. And he was mightier than the dreary tides, and went with great leaps over the listless mud. And all the sad forgotten things rejoiced, and mingled with things that were haughtier than they, and rode once more amongst the lordly shipping that was driven up and down. And out of their hideous home he took my bones, never again, I hoped, to be vexed with the ebb and flow. And with the fall of the tide he went riding down the river and turned to the southwards, and so went to his home. And my bones he scattered among many isles and along the shores of happy alien mainlands. And for a moment, while they were far asunder, my soul was almost free.

Then there arose, at the will of the moon, the assiduous flow of the tide, and it undid at once the work of the ebb, and gathered my bones from the marge of sunny isles, and gleaned them all along the mainland's shores, and went rocking northwards till it came to the mouth of the Thames, and there turned westwards its relentless face, and so went up the river and came to the hole in the mud, and into it dropped my bones; and partly the mud covered them and partly it left them white, for the mud cares not for its forsaken things.

Then the ebb came, and I saw the dead eyes of the houses and the jealousy of the other forgotten things that the storm had not carried thence.

And some more centuries passed over the ebb and flow and over the loneliness of things forgotten. And I lay there all the while in the careless grip of the mud, never wholly covered, yet never able to go free, and I longed for the great caress of the warm Earth or the comfortable lap of the Sea.

Sometimes men found my bones and buried them, but the tradition never died, and my friends' successors always brought them back. At last the barges went no more, and there were fewer lights; shaped timbers no longer floated down the fair-way, and there came instead old wind-uprooted trees in all their natural simplicity.

At last I was aware that somewhere near me a blade of grass was growing, and the moss began to appear all over the dead houses. One day some thistle-down went drifting over the river.

For some years I watched these signs attentively, until I became certain that London was passing away. Then I hoped once more, and all along both banks of the river there was anger among the lost things that anything should dare to hope upon the forsaken mud. Gradually the horrible houses crumbled, until the poor dead things that never had had life got decent burial among the weeds and moss. At last the may appeared and the convolvulus. Finally, the wild rose stood up over mounds that had been wharves and warehouses. Then I knew that the cause of Nature had triumphed, and London had passed away.

The last man in London came to the wall by the river, in an ancient cloak that was one of those that once my friends had worn and peered over the edge to see that I still was there. Then he went, and I never saw men again: they had passed away with London.

A few days after the last man had gone the birds came into London, all the birds that sing. When they first saw me they all looked sideways at me, then they went away a little and spoke among themselves.

"He only sinned against Man," they said; "it is not our quarrel."

"Let us be kind to him," they said.

Then they hopped nearer me and began to sing. It was the time of the rising of the dawn, and from both banks of the river, and from the sky, and from the thickets that were once the streets, hundreds of birds were singing. As the light increased the birds sang more and more; they grew thicker and thicker in the air above my head, till there were thousands of them singing there, and then millions, and at last I could see nothing but a host of flickering wings with the sunlight on them, and little gaps of sky. Then when there was nothing to be heard in London but the myraid notes of that exultant song, my soul rose up from the bones in the hole in the mud and began to climb up the song heavenwards. And it seemed that a laneway opened amongst the wings of the birds, and it went up and up, and one of the smaller gates of Paradise stood ajar at the end of it. And then I knew by a sign that the mud should receive me no more, for suddenly I found that I could weep.

At this moment I opened my eyes in bed in a house in London, and outside some sparrows were twittering in a tree in the light of the radiant morning; and there were tears still wet upon my face, for one's restraint is feeble while one sleeps. But I arose and opened the window wide, and, stretching my hands out over the little garden, I blessed the birds whose song had woken me up from the troubled and terrible centuries of my dream.

The Little City

I was in the pre-destined 11.8 from Goraghwood to Drogheda, when I suddenly saw the city. It was a little city in a valley, and only seemed to have a little smoke, and the sun caught the smoke and turned it golden, so that it looked like an old Italian picture where angels walk in the foreground and the rest is a blaze of gold. And beyond, as one could tell by the lie of the land, although one could not see through the golden smoke, I knew that there lay the paths of the roving ships.

All round there lay a patchwork of small fields all over the slopes of the hills, and the snow had come upon them tentatively, but already the birds of the waste had moved to the sheltered places for every omen boded more to fall. Far away some little hills blazed like an aureate bulwark broken off by age and fallen from the earthward rampart of Paradise. And aloof and dark the mountains stared unconcernedly seawards.

And when I saw those grey and watchful mountains, sitting where they sat while the cities of the civilizations of Araby and Asia arose like crocuses, and like crocuses fell, I wondered for how long there would be smoke in the valley and little fields on the hills.

The Highwayman

Tom o' the Roads had ridden his last ride, and was now alone in the night. From where he was, a man might see the white recumbent sheep and the black outline of the lonely downs, and the grey line of the farther and lonelier downs beyond them; or in hollows far below him, out of the pitiless wind, he might see the grey smoke of hamlets arising from black valleys. But all alike was black to the eyes of Tom, and all the sounds were silence in his ears; only his soul struggled to slip from the iron chains and to pass southwards into Paradise. And the wind blew and blew.

For Tom to-night had nought but the wind to ride; they had taken his true black horse on the day when they took from him the green fields and the sky, men's voices and the laughter of women, and had left him alone with chains about his neck to swing in the wind for ever. And the wind blew and blew.

But the soul of Tom o' the Roads was nipped by the cruel chains, and whenever it struggled to escape it was beaten backwards into the iron collar by the wind that blows from Paradise from the south. And swinging there by the neck, there fell away old sneers from off his lips, and scoffs that he had long since scoffed at God fell from his tongue, and there rotted old bad lusts out of his heart, and from his fingers the stains of deeds that were evil; and they all fell to the ground and grew there in pallid rings and clusters. And when these ill things had all fallen away, Tom's soul was clean again, as his early love had found it, a long while since in spring; and it swung up there in the wind with the bones of Tom, and with his old torn coat and rusty chains.

And the wind blew and blew.

And ever and anon the souls of the sepulchred, coming from consecrated acres, would go by beating up wind to Paradise past the Gallows Tree and past the soul of Tom, that might not go free.

Night after night Tom watched the sheep upon the downs with empty hollow sockets, till his dead hair grew and covered his poor dead face, and hid the shame of it from the sheep. And the wind blew and blew.

Sometimes on gusts of the wind came some one's tears, and beat and beat against the iron chains, but could not rust them through. And the wind blew and blew.

And every evening all the thoughts that Tom had ever uttered came flocking in from doing their work in the world, the work that may not cease, and sat along the gallows branches and chirruped to the soul of Tom, the soul that might not go free. All the thoughts that he had ever uttered! And the evil thoughts rebuked the soul that bore them because they might not die. And all those that he had uttered the most furtively, chirruped the loudest and the shrillest in the branches all the night.

And all the thoughts that Tom had ever thought about himself now pointed at the wet bones and mocked at the old torn coat. But the thoughts that he had had of others were the only companions that his soul had to soothe it in the night as it swung to and fro. And they twittered to the soul and cheered the poor dumb thing that could have dreams no more, till there came a murderous thought and drove them all away.

And the wind blew and blew.

Paul, Archbishop of Alois and Vayence, lay in his white sepulchre of marble, facing full to the southwards towards Paradise. And over his tomb was sculptured the Cross of Christ, that his soul might have repose. No wind howled here as it howled in lonely tree-tops up upon the downs, but came with gentle breezes, orchard scented, over the low lands from Paradise from the southwards, and played about forget-me-nots and grasses in the consecrated land where lay the Reposeful round the sepulchre of Paul, Archbishop of Alois and Vayence. Easy it was for a man's soul to pass from such a sepulchre, and, flitting low over remembered fields, to come upon the garden lands of Paradise and find eternal ease.

And the wind blew and blew.

In a tavern of foul repute three men were lapping gin. Their names were Joe and Will and the gypsy Puglioni; no other names had they, for of whom their fathers were they had no knowledge, but only dark suspicions.

Sin had caressed and stroked their faces often with its paws, but the face of Puglioni Sin had kissed all over the mouth and chin. Their food was robbery and their pastime murder. All of them had incurred the sorrow of God and the enmity of man. They sat at a table with a pack of cards before them, all greasy with the marks of cheating thumbs. And they whispered to one another over their gin, but so low that the landlord of the tavern at the other end of the room could hear only muffled oaths, and knew not by Whom they swore or what they said.

These three were the staunchest friends that ever God had given unto a man. And he to whom their friendship had been given had nothing else besides, saving some bones that swung in the wind and rain, and an old torn coat and iron chains, and a soul that might not go free.

But as the night wore on the three friends left their gin and stole away, and crept down to that graveyard where rested in his sepulchre Paul, Archbishop of Alois and Vayence. At the edge of the graveyard, but outside the consecrated ground, they dug a hasty grave, two digging while one watched in the wind and rain. And the worms that crept in the unhallowed ground wondered and waited.

And the terrible hour of midnight came upon them with its fears, and found them still beside the place of tombs. And the three friends trembled at the horror of such an hour in such a place, and shivered in the wind and drenching rain, but still worked on. And the wind blew and blew.

Soon they had finished. And at once they left the hungry grave with all its worms unfed, and went away over the wet fields stealthily but in haste, leaving the place of tombs behind them in the midnight. And as they went they shivered, and each man as he shivered cursed the rain aloud. And so they came to the spot where they had hidden a ladder and a lantern. There they held long debate whether they should light the lantern, or whether they should go without it for fear of the King's men. But in the end it seemed to them better that they should have the light of their lantern, and risk being taken by the King's men and hanged, than that they should come suddenly face to face in the darkness with whatever one might come face to face with a little after midnight about the Gallows Tree.

On three roads in England whereon it was not the wont of folk to go their ways in safety, travellers to-night went unmolested. But the three friends, walking several paces wide of the King's highway, approached the Gallows Tree, and Will carried the lantern and Joe the ladder, but Puglioni carried a great sword where-with to do the work which must be done. When they came close, they saw how bad was the case with Tom, for little remained of that fine figure of a man and nothing at all of his great resolute spirit, only as they came they thought they heard a whimpering cry like the sound of a thing that was caged and unfree.

To and fro, to and fro in the winds swung the bones and the soul of Tom, for the sins that he had sinned on the King's highway against the laws of the King; and with shadows and a lantern through the darkness, at the peril of their lives, came the three friends that his soul had won before it swung in chains. Thus the seeds of Tom's own soul that he had sown all his life had grown into a Gallows Tree that bore in season iron chains in clusters; while the careless seeds that he had strewn here and there, a kindly jest and a few merry words, had grown into the triple friendship that would not desert his bones.

Then the three set the ladder against the tree, and Puglioni went up with his sword in his right hand, and at the top of it he reached up and began to hack at the neck below the iron collar. Presently, the bones and the old coat and the soul of Tom fell down with a rattle, and a moment afterwards his head that had watched so long alone swung clear from the swinging chain. These things Will and Joe gathered up, and Puglioni came running down his ladder, and they heaped upon its rungs the terrible remains of their friend, and hastened away wet through with the rain, with the fear of phantoms in their hearts and horror lying before them on the ladder. By two o'clock they were down again in the valley out of the bitter wind, but they went on past the open grave into the graveyard all among the tombs, with their lantern and their ladder and the terrible thing upon it, which kept their friendship still. Then these three, that had robbed the Law of its due and proper victim, still sinned on for what was still their friend, and levered out the marble slabs from the sacred sepulchre of Paul, Archbishop of Alois and Vayence. And from it they took the very bones of the Archbishop himself, and carried them away to the eager grave that they had left, and put them in and shovelled back the earth. But all that lay on the ladder they placed, with a few tears, within the great white sepulchre under the Cross of Christ, and put back the marble slabs.

Thence the soul of Tom, arising hallowed out of sacred ground, went at dawn down the valley, and, lingering a little about his mother's cottage and old haunts of childhood, passed on and came to the wide lands beyond the clustered homesteads. There, there met with it all the kindly thoughts that the soul of Tom had ever had, and they flew and sang beside it all the way southwards, until at last, with singing all about it, it came to Paradise.

But Will and Joe and the gypsy Puglioni went back to their gin, and robbed and cheated again in the tavern of foul repute, and knew not that in their sinful lives they had sinned one sin at which the Angels smiled.

In the Twilight

The lock was quite crowded with boats when we capsized. I went down backwards for some few feet before I started to swim, then I came spluttering upwards towards the light; but, instead of reaching the surface, I hit my head against the keel of a boat and went down again. I struck out almost at once and came up, but before I reached the surface my head crashed against a boat for the second time, and I went right to the bottom. I was confused and thoroughly frightened. I was desperately in need of air, and knew that if I hit a boat for the third time I should never see the surface again. Drowning is a horrible death, notwithstanding all that has been said to the contrary. My past life never occurred to my mind, but I thought of many trivial things that I might not do or see again if I were drowned. I swam up in a slanting direction, hoping to avoid the boat that I had struck. Suddenly I saw all the boats in the lock quite clearly just above me, and every one of their curved varnished planks and the scratches and chips upon their keels. I saw several gaps among the boats where I might have swam up to the surface, but it did not seem worth while to try and get there, and I had forgotten why I wanted to. Then all the people leaned over the sides of their boats: I saw the light flannel suits of the men and the coloured flowers in the women's hats, and I noticed details of their dresses quite distinctly. Everybody in the boats was looking down at me; then they all said to one another, "We must leave him now," and they and the boats went away; and there was nothing above me but the river and the sky, and on either side of me were the green weeds that grew in the mud, for I had somehow sunk back to the bottom again. The river as it flowed by murmured not unpleasantly in my ears, and the rushes seemed to be whispering quite softly among themselves. Presently the murmuring of the river took the form of words, and I heard it say, "We must go on to the sea; we must leave him now."

Then the river went away, and both its banks; and the rushes whispered, "Yes, we must leave him now." And they too departed, and I was left in a great emptiness staring up at the blue sky. Then the great sky bent over me, and spoke quite softly like a kindly nurse soothing some little foolish child, and the sky said, "Goodbye. All will be well. Goodbye." And I was sorry to lose the blue sky, but the sky went away. Then I was alone, with nothing round about me; I could see no light, but it was not dark—there was just absolutely nothing, above me and below me and on every side. I thought that perhaps I was dead, and that this might be eternity; when suddenly some great southern hills rose up all round about me, and I was lying on the warm, grassy slope of a valley in England. It was a valley that I had known well when I was young, but I had not seen it now for many years. Beside me stood the tall flower of the mint; I saw the sweet-smelling thyme flower and one or two wild strawberries. There came up to me from fields below me the beautiful smell of hay, and there was a break in the voice of the cuckoo. There was a feeling of summer and of evening and of lateness and of Sabbath in the air; the sky was calm and full of a strange colour, and the sun was low; the bells in the church in the village were all a-ring, and the chimes went wandering with echoes up the valley towards the sun, and whenever the echoes died a new chime was born. And all the people of the village walked up a stone-paved path under a black oak porch and went into the church, and the chimes stopped and the people of the village began to sing, and the level sunlight shone on the white tombstones that stood all round the church. Then there was a stillness in the village, and shouts and laughter came up from the valley no more, only the occasional sound of the organ and of song. And the blue butterflies, those that love the chalk, came and perched themselves on the tall grasses, five or six sometimes on a single piece of grass, and they closed their wings and slept, and the grass bent a little beneath them. And from the woods along the tops of the hills the rabbits came hopping out and nibbled the grass, and hopped a little further and nibbled again, and the large daisies closed their petals up and the birds began to sing.

Then the hills spoke, all the great chalk hills that I loved, and with a deep and solemn voice they said, "We have come to you to say Goodbye."

Then they all went away, and there was nothing again all round about me upon every side. I looked everywhere for something on which to rest the eye. Nothing. Suddenly a low grey sky swept over me and a moist air met my face; a great plain rushed up to me from the edge of the clouds; on two sides it touched the sky, and on two sides between it and the clouds a line of low hills lay. One line of hills brooded grey in the distance, the other stood a patchwork of little square green fields, with a few white cottages about it. The plain was an archipelago of a million islands each about a yard square or less, and every one of them was red with heather. I was back on the Bog of Allen again after many years, and it was just the same as ever, though I had heard that they were draining it. I was with an old friend whom I was glad to see again, for they had told me that he died some years ago. He seemed strangely young, but what surprised me most was that he stood upon a piece of bright green moss which I had always learned to think would never bear. I was glad, too, to see the old bog again and all the lovely things that grew there—the scarlet mosses and the green mosses and the firm and friendly heather, and the deep silent water. I saw a little stream that wandered vaguely through the bog, and little white shells down in the clear depths of it; I saw, a little way off, one of the great pools where no islands are, with rushes round its borders, where the ducks love to come. I looked long at that untroubled world of heather, and then I looked at the white cottages on the hill, and saw the grey smoke curling from their chimneys and knew that they burned turf there, and longed for the smell of burning turf again. And far away there arose and came nearer the weird cry of wild and happy voices, and a flock of geese appeared that was coming from the northward. Then their cries blended into one great voice of exultation, the voice of freedom, the voice of Ireland, the voice of the Waste; and the voice said "Goodbye to you. Goodbye!" and passed away into the distance; and as it passed, the tame geese on the farms cried out to their brothers up above them that they were free. Then the hills went away, and the bog and the sky went with them, and I was alone again, as lost souls are alone.

Then there grew up beside me the red brick buildings of my first school and the chapel that adjoined it. The fields a little way off were full of boys in white flannels playing cricket. On the asphalt playing ground, just by the schoolroom windows, stood Agamemnon, Achilles, and Odysseus, with their Argives armed behind them; but Hector stepped down out of a ground-floor window, and in the schoolroom were all Priam's sons and the Achæans and fair Helen; and a little farther away the Ten Thousand drifted across the playground, going up into the heart of Persia to place Cyrus on his brother's throne. And the boys that I knew called to me from the fields, and said "Goodbye," and they and the fields went away; and the Ten Thousand said "Goodbye," each file as they passed me marching swiftly, and they too disappeared. And Hector and Agamemnon said "Goodbye," and the host of the Argives and of the Achæans; and they all went away and the old school with them, and I was alone again.

The next scene that filled the emptiness was rather

dim: I was being led by my nurse along a little footpath over a common in Surrey. She was quite young. Close by a band of gypsies had lit their fire, near them their romantic caravan stood unhorsed, and the horse cropped grass beside it. It was evening, and the gypsies muttered round their fire in a tongue unknown and strange. Then they all said in English, "Goodbye." And the evening and the common and the camp-fire went away. And instead of this a white highway with darkness and stars below it that led into darkness and stars, but at the near end of the road were common fields and gardens, and there I stood close to a large number of people, men and women. And I saw a man walking alone down the road away from me towards the darkness and the stars, and all the people called him by his name, and the man would not hear them, but walked on down the road, and the people went on calling him by his name. But I became irritated with the man because he would not stop or turn round when so many people called him by his name, and it was a very strange name. And I became weary of hearing the strange name so very often repeated, so that I made a great effort to call him, that he might listen and that the people might stop repeating this strange name. And with the effort I opened my eyes wide, and the name that the people called was my own name, and I lay on the river's bank with men and women bending over me, and my hair was wet.

The Ghosts

The argument that I had with my brother in his great lonely house will scarcely interest my readers. Not those, at least, whom I hope may be attracted by the experiment that I undertook, and by the strange things that befell me in that hazardous region into which so lightly and so ignorantly I allowed my fancy to enter. It was at Oneleigh that I had visited him.

Now Oneleigh stands in a wide isolation, in the midst of a dark gathering of old whispering cedars. They nod their heads together when the North Wind comes, and nod again and agree, and furtively grow still again, and say no more awhile. The North Wind is to them like a nice problem among wise old men; they nod their heads over it, and mutter about it all together. They know much, those cedars, they have been there so long. Their grandsires knew Lebanon, and the grandsires of these were the servants of the King of Tyre and came to Solomon's court. And amidst these black-haired children of grey-headed Time stood the old house of Oneleigh. I know not how many centuries had lashed against it their evanescent foam of years; but it was still unshattered, and all about it were the things of long ago, as cling strange growths to some sea-defying rock. Here, like the shells of long-dead limpets, was armour that men encased themselves in long ago; here, too, were tapestries of many colours, beautiful as seaweed; no modern flotsam ever drifted hither, no early Victorian furniture, no electric light. The great trade routes that littered the years with empty meat tins and cheap novels were far from here. Well, well, the centuries will shatter it and drive its fragments on to distant shores.

Meanwhile, while it yet stood, I went on a visit there to my brother, and we argued about ghosts. My brother's intelligence on this subject seemed to me to be in need of correction. He mistook things imagined for things having an actual existence; he argued that second-hand evidence of persons having seen ghosts proved ghosts to exist. I said that even if they had seen ghosts, this was no proof at all; nobody believes that there are red rats, though there is plenty of first-hand evidence of men having seen them in delirium. Finally, I said I would see ghosts myself, and continued to argue against their actual existence. So I collected a handful of cigars and drank several cups of very strong tea, and went without my dinner, and retired into a room where there was dark oak and all the chairs were covered with tapestry; and my brother went to bed bored with our argument, and trying hard to dissuade me from making myself uncomfortable. All the way up the old stairs as I stood at the bottom of them, and as his candle went winding up and up, I heard him still trying to persuade me to have supper and go to bed.

It was a windy winter, and outside the cedars were muttering I know not what about; but I think that they were Tories of a school long dead, and were troubled about something new. Within, a great damp log upon the fireplace began to squeak and sing, and struck up a whining tune, and a tall flame stood up over it and beat time, and all the shadows crowded round and began to dance. In distant corners old masses of darkness sat still like chaperones and never moved. Over there, in the darkest part of the room, stood a door that was always locked. It led into the hall, but no one ever used it; near that door something had happened once of which the family are not proud. We do not speak of it. There in the firelight stood the venerable forms of the old chairs; the hands that had made their tapestries lay far beneath the soil, the needles with which they wrought were many separate flakes of rust. No one wove now in that old room—no one but the assiduous ancient spiders who, watching by the deathbed of the things of yore, worked shrouds to hold their dust. In shrouds about the cornices already lay the heart of the oak wainscot that the worm had eaten out.

Surely at such an hour, in such a room, a fancy already excited by hunger and strong tea might see the ghosts of former occupants. I expected nothing less. The fire flickered and the shadows danced, memories of strange historic things rose vividly in my mind; but midnight chimed solemnly from a seven-foot clock, and nothing happened. My imagination would not be hurried, and the chill that is with the small hours had come upon me, and I had nearly abandoned myself to sleep, when in the hall adjoining there arose the rustling of silk dresses that I had waited for and expected. Then there entered two by two the high-born ladies and their gallants of Jacobean times. They were little more than shadows—very dignified shadows, and almost indistinct; but you have all read ghost stories before, you have all seen in museums the dresses of those times— there is little need to describe them; they entered, several of them, and sat down on the old chairs, perhaps a little carelessly considering the value of the tapestries. Then the rustling of their dresses ceased.

Well—I had seen ghosts, and was neither frightened nor convinced that ghosts existed. I was about to get up out of my chair and go to bed, when there came a sound of pattering in the hall, a sound of bare feet coming over the polished floor, and every now and then a foot would slip and I heard claws scratching along the wood as some four-footed thing lost and regained its balance. I was not frightened, but uneasy. The pattering came straight towards the room that I was in, then I heard the sniffing of expectant nostrils; perhaps "uneasy" was not the most suitable word to describe my feelings then. Suddenly a herd of black creatures larger than bloodhounds came galloping in; they had large pendulous ears, their noses were to the ground sniffing, they went up to the lords and ladies of long ago and fawned about them disgustingly. Their eyes were horribly bright, and ran down to great depths. When I looked into them I knew suddenly what these creatures were, and I was afraid. They were the sins, the filthy, immortal sins of those courtly men and women.

How demure she was, the lady that sat near me on an old-world chair—how demure she was, and how fair, to have beside her with its jowl upon her lap a sin with such cavernous red eyes, a clear case of murder. And you, yonder lady with the golden hair, surely not you— and yet that fearful beast with the yellow eyes slinks from you to yonder courtier there, and whenever one drives it away it slinks back to the other. Over there a lady tries to smile as she strokes the loathsome furry head of another's sin, but one of her own is jealous and intrudes itself under her hand. Here sits an old nobleman with his grandson on his knee, and one of the great black sins of the grandfather is licking the child's face and has made the child its own. Sometimes a ghost would move and seek another chair, but always his pack of sins would move behind him. Poor ghosts, poor ghosts! how many flights they must have attempted for two hundred years from their hated sins, how many excuses they must have given for their presence, and the sins were with them still—and still unexplained. Suddenly one of them seemed to scent my living blood, and bayed horribly, and all the others left their ghosts at once and dashed up to the sin that had given tongue. The brute had picked up my scent near the door by which I had entered, and they moved slowly nearer to me sniffing along the floor, and uttering every now and then their fearful cry. I saw that the whole thing had gone too far. But now they had seen me, now they were all about me, they sprang up trying to reach my throat; and whenever their claws touched me, horrible thoughts came into my mind and unutterable desires dominated my heart. I planned bestial things as these creatures leaped around me, and planned them with a masterly cunning. A great red-eyed murder was among the foremost of those furry things from whom I feebly strove to defend my throat. Suddenly it seemed to me good that I should kill my brother. It seemed important to me that I should not risk being punished. I knew where a revolver was kept; after I had shot him, I would dress the body up and put flour on the face like a man that had been acting as a ghost. It would be very simple. I would say that he had frightened me—and the servants had heard us talking about ghosts. There were one or two trivialities that would have to be arranged, but nothing escaped my mind. Yes, it seemed to me very good that I should kill my brother as I looked into the red depths of this creature's eyes. But one last effort as they dragged me down—"If two straight lines cut one another," I said, "the opposite angles are equal. Let AB, CD, cut one another at E, then the angles CEA, CEB equal two right angles (prop. xiii.). Also CEA, AED equal two right angles."

I moved towards the door to get the revolver; a hideous exultation arose among the beasts. "But the angle CEA is common, therefore AED equals CEB. In the same way CEA equals DEB. *Q.E.D.*" It was proved. Logic and reason reestablished themselves in my mind, there were no dark hounds of sin, the tapestried chairs were empty. It seemed to me an inconceivable thought that a man should murder his brother.

The Doom of
La Traviata

Evening stole up out of mysterious lands and came
down on the streets of Paris, and the things of the day
withdrew themselves and hid away, and the beautiful
city was strangely altered, and with it the hearts of men.
And with lights and music, and in silence and in the
dark, the other life arose, the life that knows the night,
and dark cats crept from the houses and moved to silent
places, and dim streets became haunted with dusk
shapes. At this hour in a mean house, near to the
Moulin Rouge, La Traviata died; and her death was
brought to her by her own sins, and not by the years of
God. But the soul of La Traviata drifted blindly about
the streets where she had sinned till it struck against the
wall of Notre Dame de Paris. Thence it rushed upwards,
as the sea mist when it beats against a cliff, and
streamed away to Paradise, and was there judged. And
it seemed to me, as I watched from my place of dreaming, when La Traviata came and stood before the seat
of judgment, that clouds came rushing up from the far
Paradisal hills and gathered together over the head of
God, and became one black cloud; and the clouds
moved swiftly as shadows of the night when a lantern
is swung in the hand, and more and more clouds
rushed up, and ever more and more, and, as they
gathered, the cloud a little above the head of God became no larger, but only grew blacker and blacker.
And the halos of the saints settled lower upon their
heads and narrowed and became pale, and the singing
of the choirs of the seraphim faltered and sunk low, and
the converse of the blessed suddenly ceased. Then a
stern look came into the face of God, so that the

seraphim turned away and left Him, and the saints. Then God commanded, and seven great angels rose up slowly through the clouds that carpet Paradise, and there was pity on their faces, and their eyes were closed. Then God pronounced judgment, and the lights of Paradise went out, and the azure crystal windows that look towards the world, and the windows rouge and verd, became dark and colourless, and I saw no more. Presently the seven great angels came out by one of Heaven's gates and set their faces Hellwards, and four of them carried the young soul of La Traviata, and one of them went on before and one of them followed behind. These six trod with mighty strides the long and dusty road that is named the Way of the Damned. But the seventh flew above them all the way, and the light of the fires of Hell that was hidden from the six by the dust of that dreadful road flared on the feathers of his breast.

Presently the seven angels, as they swept Hellwards, uttered speech.

"She is very young," they said; and "She is very beautiful," they said; and they looked long at the soul of La Traviata, looking not at the stains of sin, but at that portion of her soul wherewith she had loved her sister a long while dead, who flitted now about an orchard on one of Heaven's hills with a low sunlight ever on her face, who communed daily with the saints when they passed that way going to bless the dead from Heaven's utmost edge. And as they looked long at the beauty of all that remained beautiful in her soul they said: "It is but a young soul"; and they would have taken her to one of Heaven's hills, and would there have given her a cymbal and a dulcimer, but they knew that the Paradisal gates were clamped and barred against La Traviata. And they would have taken her to a valley in the world where there were a great many flowers and a loud sound of streams, where birds were singing always and church bells rang on Sabbaths, only this they durst not do. So they swept onward nearer and nearer Hell. But when they were come quite close and the glare was on their faces, and they saw the gates already divide and prepare to open outwards, they said: "Hell is a terrible city, and she is tired of cities"; then suddenly they dropped her by the side of the road, and wheeled and flew away. But into a great pink flower that was horrible and lovely grew the soul of La Traviata; and it had in it two eyes but no eyelids, and it stared constantly into the faces of all the passers-by that went along the dusty road to Hell; and the flower grew in the glare of the lights of Hell, and withered but could not die; only, one petal turned back towards the heavenly hills as an ivy leaf turns outwards to the day, and in the soft and silvery light of Paradise it withered not nor faded, but heard at times the commune of the saints coming murmuring from the distance, and sometimes caught the scent of orchards wafted from the heavenly hills, and felt a faint breeze cool it every evening at the hour when the saints to Heaven's edge went forth to bless the dead.

But the Lord arose with His sword, and scattered His disobedient angels as a thresher scatters chaff.

A Narrow Escape

It was underground.

In that dank cavern down below Belgrave Square the walls were dripping. But what was that to the magician? It was secrecy that he needed, not dryness. There he pondered upon the trend of events, shaped destinies and concocted magical brews.

For the last few years the serenity of his ponderings had been disturbed by the noise of the motor-bus; while to his keen ears there came the earthquake-rumble, far off, of the train in the tube, going down Sloane Street; and what he heard of the world above his head was not to its credit.

He decided one evening over his evil pipe, down there in his dank chamber, that London had lived long enough, had abused its opportunities, had gone too far, in fine, with its civilisation. And so he decided to wreck it.

Therefore he beckoned up his acolyte from the weedy end of the cavern, and, "Bring me," he said, "the heart of the toad that dwelleth in Arabia and by the mountains of Bethany." The acolyte slipped away by the hidden door, leaving that grim old man with his frightful pipe, and whither he went who knows but the gipsy people, or by what path he returned; but within a year he stood in the cavern again, slipping secretly in by the trap while the old man smoked, and he brought with him a little fleshy thing that rotted in a casket of pure gold.

"What is it?" the old man croaked.

"It is," said the acolyte, "the heart of the toad that dwelt once in Arabia and by the mountains of Bethany."

The old man's crooked fingers closed on it, and he blessed the acolyte with his rasping voice and claw-like hand uplifted; the motor-bus rumbled above on its endless journey; far off the train shook Sloane Street.

"Come," said the old magician, "it is time." And there and then they left the weedy cavern, the acolyte carrying cauldron, gold poker and all things needful, and went abroad in the light. And very wonderful the old man looked in his silks.

Their goal was the outskirts of London; the old man strode in front and the acolyte ran behind him, and there was something magical in the old man's stride alone, without his wonderful dress, the cauldron and wand, the hurrying acolyte and the small gold poker.

Little boys jeered till they caught the old man's eye. So there went on through London this strange procession of two, too swift for any to follow. Things seemed worse up there than they did in the cavern, and the further they got on their way towards London's outskirts the worse London got. "It is time," said the old man, "surely."

And so they came at last to London's edge and a small hill watching it with a mournful look. It was so mean that the acolyte longed for the cavern; dank though it was and full of terrible sayings that the old man said when he slept.

They climbed the hill and put the cauldron down, and put there in the necessary things, and lit a fire of herbs that no chemist will sell nor decent gardener grow, and stirred the cauldron with the golden poker. The magician retired a little apart and muttered, then he strode back to the cauldron and, all being ready, suddenly opened the casket and let the fleshy thing fall in to boil.

Then he made spells, then he flung up his arms; the fumes from the cauldron entering in at his mind he said raging things that he had not known before and runes that were dreadful (the acolyte screamed); there he cursed London from fog to loam-pit, from zenith to the abyss, motor-bus, factory, shop, parliament, people. "Let them all perish," he said, "and London pass away, tram lines and bricks and pavement, the usurpers too long of the fields, let them all pass away and the wild hares come back, blackberry and briar-rose."

"Let it pass," he said, "pass now, pass utterly."

In the momentary silence the old man coughed, then waited with eager eyes; and the long long hum of London hummed as it always has since first the reed-huts were set up by the river, changing its note at times but always humming, louder now than it was in years gone by, but humming night and day though its voice be cracked with age; so it hummed on.

And the old man turned him round to his trembling acolyte and terribly said as he sank into the earth: "YOU HAVE NOT BROUGHT ME THE HEART OF THE TOAD THAT DWELLETH IN ARABIA NOR BY THE MOUNTAINS OF BETHANY!"

The Lord of Cities

I came one day upon a road that wandered so aimlessly
that it was suited to my mood, so I followed it, and it
led me presently among deep woods. Somewhere in
the midst of them Autumn held his court, sitting
wreathed with gorgeous garlands; and it was the day
before his annual festival of the Dance of Leaves, the
courtly festival upon which hungry Winter rushes mob-
like, and there arise the furious cries of the North
Wind triumphing, and all the splendour and grace of
the woods is gone, and Autumn flees away, discrowned
and forgotten, and never again returns. Other Autumns
arise, other Autumns, and fall before other Winters. A
road led away to the left, but my road went straight on.
The road to the left had a trodden appearance; there
were wheel tracks on it, and it seemed the correct way
to take. It looked as if no one could have any business
with the road that led straight on and up the hill. There-
fort I went straight on and up the hill; and here and
there on the road grew blades of grass undisturbed in
the repose and hush that the road had earned from
going up and down the world; for you can go by this
road, as you can go by all roads, to London, to Lincoln,
to the North of Scotland, to the West of Wales, and to
Wrellisford where roads end. Presently the woods
ended, and I came to the open fields and at the same
moment to the top of the hill, and saw the high places
of Somerset and the downs of Wilts spread out along
the horizon. Suddenly I saw underneath me the village
of Wrellisford, with no sound in its street but the voice
of the Wrellis roaring as he tumbled over a weir above
the village. So I followed my road down over the crest

181

of the hill, and the road became more languid as I descended, and less and less concerned with the cares of a highway. Here a spring broke out in the middle of it, and here another. The road never heeded. A stream ran right across it, still it straggled on. Suddenly it gave up the minimum property that a road should possess, and, renouncing its connection with High Streets, its lineage of Piccadilly, shrank to one side and became an unpretentious footpath. Then it led me to the old bridge over the stream, and thus I came to Wrellisford, and found after travelling in many lands a village with no wheel tracks in its street. On the other side of the bridge, my friend the road struggled a few yards up a grassy slope, and there ceased. Over all the village hung a great stillness, with the roar of the Wrellis cutting right across it, and there came occasionally the bark of a dog that kept watch over the broken stillness and over the sanctity of that untravelled road. That terrible and wasting fever that, unlike so many plagues, comes not from the East but from the West, the fever of hurry, had not come here—only the Wrellis hurried on his eternal quest, but it was a calm and placid hurry that gave one time for song. It was in the early afternoon, and nobody was about. Either they worked beyond the mysterious valley that nursed Wrellisford and hid it from the world, or else they secluded themselves within their old-time houses that were roofed with tiles of stone. I sat down upon the old stone bridge and watched the Wrellis, who seemed to me to be the only traveller that came from far away into this village where roads end, and passed on beyond it. And yet the Wrellis comes singing out of eternity, and tarries for a very little while in the village where roads end, and passes on into eternity again; and so surely do all that dwell in Wrellisford. I wondered as I leaned upon the bridge in what place the Wrellis would first find the sea, whether as he wound idly through meadows on his long quest he would suddenly behold him, and, leaping down over some rocky cliff, take to him at once the message of the hills. Or whether, widening slowly into some grand and tidal estuary, he would take his waste of waters to the sea and the might of the river should meet with the might of the waves, like to two Emperors clad in gleaming mail meeting midway between two hosts of war; and the little Wrellis would become a haven for returning ships and a setting-out place for adventurous men.

A little beyond the bridge there stood an old mill with a ruined roof, and a small branch of the Wrellis rushed through its emptiness shouting, like a boy playing alone in a corridor of some desolate house. The mill-wheel was gone, but there lay there still great bars and wheels and cogs, the bones of some dead industry. I know not what industry was once lord in that house, I know not what retinue of workers mourns him now; I only know who is lord there to-day in all those empty chambers. For as soon as I entered, I saw a whole wall draped with his marvellous black tapestry, without price because inimitable and too delicate to pass from hand to hand among merchants. I looked at the wonderful complexity of its infinite threads, my finger sank into it for more than an inch without feeling the touch; so black it was and so carefully wrought, sombrely covering the whole of the wall, that it might have been worked to commemorate the deaths of all that ever lived there, as indeed it was. I looked through a hole in the wall into an inner chamber where a worn-out driving band went among many wheels, and there this priceless inimitable stuff not merely clothed the walls but hung from bars and ceiling in beautiful draperies, in marvellous festoons. Nothing was ugly in this desolate house, for the busy artist's soul of its present lord had beautified everything in its desolation. It was the unmistakable work of the spider, in whose house I was, and the house was utterly desolate but for him, and silent but for the roar of the Wrellis and the shout of the little stream. Then I turned homewards; and as I went up and over the hill and lost the sight of the village, I saw the road whiten and harden and gradually broaden out till the tracks of wheels appeared; and it went afar to take the young men of Wrellisford into the wide ways of the earth—to the new West and the mysterious East, and into the troubled South.

And that night, when the house was still and sleep was far off, hushing hamlets and giving ease to cities, my fancy wandered up that aimless road and came suddenly to Wrellisford. And it seemed to me that the travelling of so many people for so many years between Wrellisford and John o' Groat's, talking to one another as they went or muttering alone, had given the road a voice. And it seemed to me that night that the road spoke to the river by Wrellisford bridge, speaking with the voice of many pilgrims. And the road said to the river: "I rest here. How is it with you?"

And the river, who is always speaking, said: "I rest nowhere from doing the Work of the World. I carry the murmur of inner lands to the sea, and to the abysses voices of the hills."

"It is I," said the road, "that do the Work of the World, and take from city to city the rumour of each. There is nothing higher than Man and the making of cities. What do you do for Man?"

And the river said: "Beauty and song are higher than Man. I carry the news seaward of the first song of the thrush after the furious retreat of winter northward, and the first timid anemone learns from me that she is safe and that spring has truly come. Oh but the song of all the birds in spring is more beautiful than Man, and the first coming of the hyacinth more delectable than his face! When spring is fallen upon the days of summer, I carry away with mournful joy at night petal by petal the rhododendron's bloom. No lit procession of purple kings is nigh so fair as that. No beautiful death of well-beloved men hath such a glory of forlornness. And I bear far away the pink and white petals of the apple-blossom's youth when the laborious time comes for his work in the world and for the bearing of apples. And I am robed each day and every night anew with the beauty of heaven, and I make lovely visions of the trees. But Man! What is Man? In the ancient parliament of the elder hills, when the grey ones speak together, they say nought of Man, but concern themselves only with their brethren the stars. Or when they wrap themselves in purple cloaks at evening, they lament some old irreparable wrong, or, uttering some mountain hymn, all mourn the set of sun."

"Your beauty," said the road, "and the beauty of the sky, and of the rhododendron blossom and of spring, live only in the mind of Man, and except in the mind of Man the mountains have no voices. Nothing is beautiful that has not been seen by Man's eye. Or if your rhododendron blossom was beautiful for a moment, it soon withered and was drowned, and spring soon passes away; beauty can only live on in the mind of Man. I bring thought into the mind of Man swiftly from distant places every day. I know the Telegraph—I know him well; he and I have walked for hundreds of miles together. There is no work in the world except for Man and the making of his cities. I take wares to and fro from city to city."

"My little stream in the field there," said the river, "used to make wares in that house for awhile once."

"Ah," said the road, "I remember, but I brought cheaper ones from distant cities. Nothing is of any importance but making cities for Man."

"I know so little about him," said the river, "but I have a great deal of work to do—I have all this water to send down to the sea; and then to-morrow or next day all the leaves of Autumn will be coming this way. It will be very beautiful. The sea is a very, very wonderful place. I know all about it; I have heard shepherd boys singing of it, and sometimes before a storm the gulls come up. It is a place all blue and shining and full of pearls, and has in it coral islands and isles of spice, and storms and galleons and the bones of Drake. The sea is much greater than Man. When I come to the sea, he will know that I have worked well for him. But I must hurry, for I have much to do. This bridge delays me a little; some day I will carry it away."

"Oh, you must not do that," said the road.

"Oh, not for a long time," said the river. "Some centuries perhaps—and I have much to do besides. There is my song to sing, for instance, and that alone is more beautiful than any noise that Man makes."

"All work is for Man," said the road, "and for the building of cities. There is no beauty or romance or mystery in the sea except for the men that sail abroad upon it, and for those that stay at home and dream of them. As for your song, it rings night and morning, year in, year out, in the ears of men that are born in Wrellisford; at night it is part of their dreams, at morning it is the voice of day, and so it becomes part of their souls. But the song is not beautiful in itself. I take these men with your song in their souls up over the edge of the valley and a long way off beyond, and I am a strong and dusty road up there, and they go with your song in their souls and turn it into music and gladden cities. But nothing is the Work of the World except work for Man."

"I wish I was quite sure about the Work of the World," said the stream; "I wish I knew for certain for whom we work. I feel almost sure that it is for the sea. He is very great and beautiful. I think that there can be no greater master than the sea. I think that some day he may be so full of romance and mystery and sound of sheep bells and murmur of mist-hidden hills, which we streams shall have brought him, that there will be no more music or beauty left in the world, and all the world will end; and perhaps the streams shall gather at the last, we all together, to the sea. Or perhaps the sea will give us at the last unto each one his own again, giving back all that he had garnered in the years—the little petals of the apple-blossom and the mourned ones of the rhododendron, and our old visions of the trees and sky; so many memories have left the hills. But who may say? For who knows the tides of the sea?"

"Be sure that it is all for Man," said the road. "For Man and the making of cities."

Something had come near on utterly silent feet.

"Peace, peace!" it said. "You disturb the queenly night, who, having come into this valley, is a guest in my dark halls. Let us have an end to this discussion."

It was the spider who spoke.

"The Work of the World is the making of cities and palaces. But it is not for Man. What is Man? He only prepares my cities for me, and mellows them. All his works are ugly, his richest tapestries are coarse and clumsy. He is a noisy idler. He only protects me from mine enemy the wind; and the beautiful work in my cities, the curving outlines and the delicate weavings, is all mine. Ten years to a hundred it takes to build a city, for five or six hundred more it mellows, and is prepared for me; then I inhabit it, and hide away all that is ugly, and draw beautiful lines about it to and fro. There is nothing so beautiful as cities and palaces; they are the loveliest places in the world, because they are the stillest, and so most like the stars. They are noisy at first, for a little, before I come to them; they have ugly corners not yet rounded off, and coarse tapestries, and then they become ready for me and my exquisite work, and are quite silent and beautiful. And there I entertain the regal nights when they come there jewelled with stars, and all their train of silence, and regale them with costly dust. Already nods, in a city that I wot of, a lonely sentinel whose lords are dead, who grows too old and sleepy to drive away the gathering silence that infests the streets; to-morrow I go to see if he be still at his post. For me Babylon was built, and rocky Tyre; and still men build my cities! All the Work of the World is the making of cities, and all of them I inherit."

The Unhappy Body

"Why do you not dance with us and rejoice with us?" they said to a certain body. And then that body made the confession of its trouble. It said: "I am united with a fierce and violent soul, that is altogether tyrannous and will not let me rest, and he drags me away from the dances of my kin to make me toil at his detestable work; and he will not let me do the little things, that would give pleasure to the folk I love, but only cares to please posterity when he has done with me and left me to the worms; and all the while he makes absurd demands of affection from those that are near to me, and is too proud even to notice any less than he demands, so that those that should be kind to me all hate me." And the unhappy body burst into tears.

And they said: "No sensible body cares for its soul. A soul is a little thing, and should not rule a body. You should drink and smoke more till he ceases to trouble you." But the body only wept, and said, "Mine is a fearful soul. I have driven him away for a little while with drink. But he will soon come back. Oh, he will soon come back!"

And the body went to bed hoping to rest, for it was drowsy with drink. But just as sleep was near it, it looked up, and there was its soul sitting on the window-sill, a misty blaze of light, and looking into the street.

"Come," said that tyrannous soul, "and look into the street."

"I have need of sleep," said the body.

"But the street is a beautiful thing," the soul said vehemently; "a hundred of the people are dreaming there."

"I am ill through want of rest," the body said.

"That does not matter," the soul said to it. "There are millions like you in the earth, and millions more to go there. The people's dreams are wandering afield; they pass the seas and the mountains of faëry, threading the intricate passes led by their souls; they come to golden temples a-ring with a thousand bells; they pass up steep streets lit by paper lanterns, where the doors are green and small; they know their way to witches' chambers and castles of enchantment; they know the spell that brings them to the causeway along the ivory mountains—on one side looking downward they behold the fields of their youth and on the other lie the radiant plains of the future. Arise and write down what the people dream."

"What reward is there for me," said the body, "if I write down what you bid me?"

"There is no reward," said the soul.

"Then I shall sleep," said the body.

And the soul began to hum an idle song sung by a young man in a fabulous land as he passed a golden city (where fiery sentinels stood), and knew that his wife was within it, though as yet but a little child, and knew by prophecy that furious wars, not yet arisen in far and unknown mountains, should roll above him with their dust and thirst before he ever came to that city again—the young man sang it as he passed the gate, and was now dead with his wife a thousand years.

"I cannot sleep for that abominable song," the body cried to the soul.

"Then do as you are commanded," the soul replied. And wearily the body took a pen again. Then the soul spoke merrily as he looked through the window. "There is a mountain lifting sheer above London, part crystal and part mist. Thither the dreamers go when the sound of the traffic has fallen. At first they scarcely dream because of the roar of it, but before midnight it stops, and turns, and ebbs with all its wrecks. Then the dreamers arise and scale the shimmering mountain, and at its summit find the galleons of dream. Thence some sail East, some West, some into the Past and some into the Future, for the galleons sail over the years as well as over the spaces, but mostly they head for the Past and the olden harbours, for thither the sighs of men are mostly turned, and the dream-ships go before them, as the merchantmen before the continual trade-winds go down the African coast. I see the galleons even now raise anchor after anchor; the stars flash by them; they slip out of the night; their prows go gleaming into the twilight of memory, and night soon lies far off, a black cloud hanging low, and faintly spangled with stars, like the harbour and shore of some low-lying land seen afar with its harbour lights."

Dream after dream that soul related as he sat there by the window. He told of tropical forests seen by unhappy men who could not escape from London, and never would—forests made suddenly wondrous by the song of some passing bird flying to unknown eeries and singing an unknown song. He saw the old men lightly dancing to the tune of elfin pipes—beautiful dances with fantastic maidens—all night on moonlit imaginary mountains; he heard far off the music of glittering Springs; he saw the fairness of blossoms of apple and may thirty years fallen; he heard old voices—old tears came glistening back; Romance sat cloked and crowned upon southern hills, and the soul knew him.

One by one he told the dreams of all that slept in that street. Sometimes he stopped to revile the body because it worked badly and slowly. Its chill fingers wrote as fast as they could, but the soul cared not for that. And so the night wore on till the soul heard tinkling in Oriental skies far footfalls of the morning.

"See now," said the soul, "the dawn that the dreamers dread. The sails of light are paling on those unwreckable galleons; the mariners that steer them slip back into fable and myth; that other sea the traffic is turning now at its ebb, and is about to hide its pallid wrecks, and to come swinging back, with its tumult, at the flow.

Already the sunlight flashes in the gulfs behind the east of the world; the gods have seen it from their palace of twilight that they built above the sunrise; they warm their hands at its glow as it streams through their gleaming arches, before it reaches the world; all the gods are there that have ever been, and all the gods that shall be; they sit there in the morning, chanting and praising Man."

"I am numb and very cold for want of sleep," said the body.

"You shall have centuries of sleep," said the soul, "but you must not sleep now, for I have seen deep meadows with purple flowers flaming tall and strange above the brilliant grass, and herds of pure white unicorns that gambol there for joy, and a river running by with a glittering galleon on it, all of gold, that goes from an unknown inland to an unknown isle of the sea to take a song from the King of Over-the-Hills to the Queen of Far-Away.

"I will sing that song to you, and you shall write it down."

"I have toiled for you for years," the body said. "Give me now but one night's rest, for I am exceeding weary."

"Oh, go and rest. I am tired of you. I am off," said the soul.

And he arose and went, we know not whither. But the body they laid in the earth. And the next night at midnight the wraiths of the dead came drifting from their tombs to felicitate that body.

"You are free here, you know," they said to their new companion.

"Now I can rest," said the body.

The Gifts of the
Gods

There was once a man who sought a boon of the gods. For peace was over the world and all things savoured of sameness, and the man was weary at heart and sighed for the tents and the warfields. Therefore he sought a boon of the ancient gods. And appearing before them he said to them, "Ancient gods; there is peace in the land where I dwell, and indeed to the uttermost parts, and we are full weary of peace. O ancient gods, grant us war!"

And the ancient gods made him a war.

And the man went forth with his sword, and behold it was even war. And the man remembered the little things that he knew, and thought of the quiet days that there used to be, and at night on the hard ground dreamed of the things of peace. And dearer and dearer grew the wonted things, the dull but easeful things of the days of peace, and remembering these he began to regret the war, and sought once more a boon of the ancient gods, and appearing before them he said: "O ancient gods; indeed but a man loves best the days of peace. Therefore take back your war and give us peace, for indeed of all your blessedness peace is best."

And the man returned again to the haunts of peace.

But in a while the man grew weary of peace, of the things that he used to know, and the savour of sameness again; and sighing again for the tents, and appearing once more to the gods, he said to them: "Ancient gods; we do not love your peace, for indeed the days are dull, and a man is best at war."

Again the gods made him a war.

And there were drums again, the smoke of campfires

again, wind in the waste again, the sound of horses at war, burning cities again, and the things that wanderers know; and the thoughts of that man went home to the ways of peace; moss upon lawns again, light on old spires again, sun upon gardens again, flowers in pleasant woods and sleep and the paths of peace.

And once more the man appeared to the ancient gods and sought from them one more boon, and said to them: "Ancient gods; indeed but the world and we are a-weary of war and long for the ancient ways and the paths of peace."

So the gods took back their war and gave him peace.

But the man took counsel one day and communed long with himself and said to himself: "Behold, the wishes I wish, which the gods grant, are not to be much desired; and if the gods should one day grant a wish and never revoke it, which is a way of the gods, I should be sorely tried because of my wish; my wishes are dangerous wishes and not to be desired."

And therefore he wrote an anonymous letter to the gods, writing: "O ancient gods; this man that hath four times troubled you with his wishes, wishing for peace and war, is a man that hath no reverence for the gods, speaking ill of them on days when they do not hear, and speaking well of them only on holy days and at the appointed hours when the gods are hearkening to prayer. Therefore grant no more wishes to this impious man."

And the days of peace wore on and there arose again from the earth, like mist in the autumn from fields that generations have ploughed, the savour of sameness again. And the man went forth one morning and appeared once more to the gods, and cried: "O ancient gods, give us but one war again, for I would be back to the camps and debateable borders of lands."

And the gods said: "We hear not well of your way of life, yea ill things have come to our hearing, so that we grant no more the wishes you wish."

On the Dry Land

Over the marshes hung the gorgeous night with all his wandering bands of nomad stars, and his whole host of still ones blinked and watched.

Over the safe dry land to eastward, grey and cold, the first clear pallor of dawn was coming, up above the heads of the immortal gods.

Then, as they neared at last the safety of the dry land, Love looked at the man whom he had led for so long through the marshes, and saw that his hair was white, for it was shining in the pallor of the dawn.

Then they stepped together on to the land, and the old man sat down weary on the grass, for they had wandered in the marshes for many years; and the light of the grey dawn widened above the heads of the gods.

And Love said to the old man, "I will leave you now."

And the old man made no answer, but wept softly.

Then Love was grieved in his little careless heart, and he said: "You must not be sorry that I go, nor yet regret me, nor care for me at all.

"I am a very foolish child, and was never kind to you, nor friendly. I never cared for your great thoughts, or for what was good in you, but perplexed you by leading you up and down the perilous marshes. And I was so heartless that, had you perished where I led you, it would have been nought to me, and I only stayed with you because you were good to play with.

"And I am cruel and altogether worthless and not such a one as any should be sorry for when I go, or one to be regretted, or even cared for at all."

And still the old man spoke not, but wept softly; and Love grieved bitterly in his kindly heart.

And Love said: "Because I am so small my strength has been concealed from you, and the evil that I have done. But my strength is great, and I have used it unjustly. Often I pushed you from the causeway through the marshes, and cared not if you drowned. Often I mocked you, and caused others to mock you. And often I led you among those that hated me, and laughed when they revenged themselves upon you.

"So weep not, for there is no kindness in my heart, but only murder and foolishness, and I am no companion for one so wise as you, but am so frivolous and silly that I laughed at your noble dreams and hindered all your deeds. See now, you have found me out, and now you will send me away, and here you will live at ease, and, undisturbed, have noble dreams of the immortal gods.

"See now, here is dawn and safety, and *there* is darkness and peril."

Still the old man wept softly.

Then Love said: "Is it thus with you?" and his voice was grave now and quiet. "Are you so troubled? Old friend of so many years, there is grief in my heart for you. Old friend of perilous ventures, I must leave you now. But I will send my brother soon to you—my little brother Death. And he will come up out of the marshes to you, and will not forsake you, but will be true to you as I have not been true."

And dawn grew brighter over the immortal gods, and the old man smiled through his tears, which glistened wondrously in the increasing light. But Love went down to the night and to the marshes, looking backward over his shoulder as he went, and smiling beautifully about his eyes. And in the marshes whereunto he went, in the midst of the gorgeous night, and under the wandering bands of nomad stars, rose shouts of laughter and the sounds of the dance.

And after a while, with his face towards the morning, Death out of the marshes came up tall and beautiful, and with a faint smile shadowy on his lips, and lifted in his arms the lonely man, being gentle with him, and, murmuring with his low deep voice an ancient song, carried him to the morning, to the gods.

The Unpasturable Fields

Thus spake the mountains: "Behold us, even us; the old ones, the grey ones, that wear the feet of Time. Time on our rocks shall break his staff and stumble: and still we shall sit majestic, even as now, hearing the sound of the sea, our old coeval sister, who nurses the bones of her children and weeps for the things she has done.

"Far, far, we stand above all things; befriending the little cities until they grow old and leave us to go among the myths.

"We are the most imperishable mountains."

And softly the clouds foregathered from far places, and crag on crag and mountain upon mountain in the likeness of Caucasus upon Himalaya came riding past the sunlight upon the backs of storms and looked down idly from their golden heights upon the crests of the mountains.

"Ye pass away," said the mountains.

And the clouds answered, as I dreamed or fancied,

"We pass away, indeed we pass away, but upon our unpasturable fields Pegasus prances. Here Pegasus gallops and browses upon song which the larks bring to him every morning from far terrestrial fields. His hoof-beats ring upon our slopes at sunrise as though our fields were of silver. And breathing the dawn-wind in dilated nostrils, with head tossed upwards and with quivering wings, he stands and stares from our tremendous heights, and snorts and sees far-future wonderful wars rage in the creases and the folds of the togas that cover the knees of the gods."

Tales Jorkens Told

Editor's Note

LORD DUNSANY also contributed to that peculiarly British sub-genre of fiction, the Club story. Tales of this sort generally consist of loosely-connected short stories in the form of tall tales told by various members of a social club. In this category, for instance, are Arthur C. Clarke's *Tales of the White Hart* and Fletcher Pratt and L. Sprague de Camp's *Tales of Gavagan's Bar*. A number of the books of P. G. Wodehouse fall into the same classification—those devoted to the doings of the young wastrels of the Drones' Club, for instance, to say nothing of that modern-day Scheherezade, Mr. Mulliner, and the tall tales he spins at the Angler's Rest.

Into such company, Mr. Joseph Jorkens fits quite comfortably. He is a familiar fixture at the Billiards Club, and, when cozily installed in his favorite chair with a whiskey-and-soda readily at hand, he will require very little baiting by that perpetual doubting Thomas, Terbut, to relate an experience of his, such as one of those which follow. . . .

L.C.

201

The Curse of the Witch

The talk had veered round to runes and curses and witches, one bleak December evening, where a few of us sat warm in easy chairs round the cheery fire of the Billiards Club.

"Do you believe in witches?" one of us said to Jorkens.

"It isn't what I believe in that matters so much," said Jorkens; "only what I have seen."

"Have you seen one?" the other man asked.

"I know how they work," he said.

"And how do they work?" we asked him.

"Well," Jorkens said, "I want to be strictly accurate. I had once a fairly good glimpse of how one of them worked, but I can't say more than that. Different witches in different countries may perhaps have various methods. And yet I doubt it: I imagine they travel more than we suppose, and meet and talk many things over. Many a blackened patch under a hedgerow may have been a meeting place for queer discussions, and the comparing of strange notes. But who knows? Who knows?"

And somehow I feared that Jorkens was about to drift from the particular to the general, and though he might have had much to say on that that could have been instructive, yet we should have got no story. "You met a witch once, Jorkens?" I asked.

"I didn't meet her," said Jorkens. "She had probably been dead three hundred years when I chanced upon her locality. But I certainly met something of her work."

And without any further stimulus of any sort from

me he gave us his story. "It's a curious thing, when I was young," he said, "there used to come on me at times an instinct such as some birds have. Swallows I mean, corncrakes, cuckoos and all those. I felt driven southwards, felt that I must migrate. So one day I started South, and kept on till I came to Spain, walking mostly. All through France, and on foot through the Pyrenees. And one day I came to a village that somehow seemed right. Nothing there jarred on me, the roofs of the small houses comforted me, quaint chimneys seemed to beckon; little old doorways looked as though in a moment that was almost trembling to come, they would break into wooden green smiles. Over it hung the lazy sunshine of Spring, on which hawks balanced lightly, and whither went up the sound of bells from below. It almost seemed to be roofed and sheltered by sunlight and fading vibrations of bells, interlaced in a dome. That's how it seemed to me, and something at once soothed my restlessness, and I went to an inn and stayed. Probably the roofs of barns in some quiet valley have the same hold on a wandering swallow. One can't say what it is.

"The inn was of course uncomfortable, I didn't mind that; the only thing I minded was that as the night went on, and a large moon rose and I wanted to get to sleep, the most infernal howling of dogs began. The room that I had been given by the old couple that owned the inn looked out from the edge of the village over a lonely moorland, and a mile away over the hills and hollows of this wild country I could see the black shape of a large house, from which the melancholy uproar came. I could not have believed that it was so far, for the sound seemed almost underneath my window, but the old innkeeper that showed me up to my room said, at the first howl, 'The hounds in the Casa Viljeros.' And he pointed with his hand out of the window to the dark shape of the house. I asked no more about it then, for my curiosity had not been aroused and excited; it sounded no more at first than the ordinary baying of hounds that

are a little disturbed or uneasy before they sleep; and
so the old man left me and went downstairs and I knew
no more than the name of the dark house where there
were hounds. Through sleepless hours while the baying
of these hounds rose into long howls, I wished a hundred times that I had questioned him, as far as my
Spanish would go. There was a horror in knowing
nothing. Even the strange story I got next day, perhaps
even the whole story, which I shall never know, might
have made that night less horrible. It was hearing those
cries going up from some terror of which I knew nothing, that made it worse than if I had known the cause.
For it was from some terror that those hounds were
howling; one after another they spoke with little uneasy
yelps, drawn out at last into one long wavering howl.
Had it been human beings shouting a mile away one
could not have heard their words, and might well have
been in the dark as to what they debated among them;
but those that have not any words in their language are
not to be so mistaken, and their tones when they speak
are as clear to Englishman or to Spaniard as to whatever roves on soft feet through open moors in the night.
So there I sat all night listening to terror, and never
knowing what the terror was. It was no use trying to
sleep, for it was not only the noise that kept me awake:
had words that I could not understand been shouted,
however close, I should have got to sleep in time. But
when one's understanding is involved, when one knows
the message but knows not why it is sent, then wonder
awakes and all one's mind is active. At first in the
silence that followed the long howls I thought they had
finished and that the terror was over; but always as
soon as a few seconds had passed a low whimper would
come quavering over the moor, then another, and then
another a little louder, and then again the long cry
burdened with terror. Separate voices at first, and I
even tried to count them; but an hour or so after midnight, as though their forebodings had gathered force
and accumulated, the yelps and whimperings all drew

together, and rippled into a howl in which every voice was wailing. Nothing stirred on the grey moor, nobody entered or left the dark house; the hounds howled on and on, voicing their fear of a mystery to which I had no key. And even when dawn at last lifted a little of the weight of foreboding, by changing the shape of the scene over which it had brooded so long, bringing hills into view that one had not seen before, and taking away a frown from the faces of others; even then the terrified hounds, though weary of howling, were whimpering mournfully in the early light.

"What was it? What was that terror of which they told so unmistakably? Before bright morning came I may have slept a little; however that be, as soon as the old man called me, and afterwards as I had breakfast with him and his wife, I asked him for all he could tell of the house called Casa Viljeros; and on the evening of the same day I talked to the Americans who had bought the house, sitting for an hour with them over a few cocktails at the hotel in the town ten miles away, and getting from them pretty well all they knew; and I talked a bit with the gardener at the house; I got everybody's story except that of the Viljeros family, who from the old Marquis downwards would say never a word. And from all I heard I put this tale together.

"Nobody knew the age of Casa Viljeros. It was not like an English house, of which people say Queen Anne, Queen Elizabeth, or King Stephen: nobody knew. And the family of Viljeros was far older than the house. Their grand old motto stood out in stone over the door, 'Never the Moors.' It meant that the Moors should never hold Spain; and whatever topic the family might discuss, especially if they talked of the Government's policy, as they sometimes did in the evening, the old Marquis nearly always brought it round to that policy of his family, often ending the discussion for the night with the very words of the motto. And the time came, so the gardener said, when all the money was gone. The Marquis had little concerned himself with it when it was there, and could hardly believe it was not there: the wealth of a hidalgo seemed too natural to boast of, even in thought, and too much a part of his natural state to be gone while he still lived. And yet it was gone.

"But that his very house should go, and such a house as Casa Viljeros, was to him so utterly terrible, that he did not sell it as other men sell their houses, showing which is the key of the front door and which the key of the cellar, but kept one thing untold.

"And the Americans came, the family of Stolger. The business must have been done mostly by letter, for when first the gardener saw them they came into the house and the old family went out after little more than an hour. There were six of them, Gateward Stolger and his wife, Hendrik the eldest son, about twenty-five, two daughters and Easel, a boy of about sixteen. They all walked into the house; and there was the old Marquis, still there with his daughters, clinging to the home to the very last moment. Gateward Stolger had once seen the house from the outside, years ago on a holiday; but none of the Stolgers had ever been inside it. The money had been paid and the queer hurried bargain concluded, and nothing remained to be done but to show the new owners the way upstairs, and to tell them which was the boudoir and which was the library, and one other thing, that was never told them. The Stolgers had bought it lock, stock and barrel; furniture, sheets and everything; and had the idea of hunting there during the winter, and had brought their own hounds with them, the hounds I heard.

"And so the old hidalgo showed them round, with a great sombre politeness. They went from room to room; and, whatever glamour was hoarded there for the ancient Spanish family, the Americans saw none they would care to sit in till they came to the great library. Against this they could say nothing, indeed for some moments they could not speak at all; that splendid piece of the past merely held them spellbound. Evening was coming on and the room was dim: down the middle of the long room you saw the gloaming, and on either side the darkness of old carved wood and great shadows; it passed through the mind of one of them that they looked on a piece of the very history of Spain set in a strange darkness. One more room the old Marquis showed them, and that was all. And then the eldest of his two daughters spoke to him. 'Won't you tell them about . . . ?' she said.

" 'Oh, yes,' he said at once, 'the laundry.' And he began to tell the Americans where that was; and the daughter said no more; and yet there remained an expectancy on her face, a listening to every word that her father said, a hope each time he spoke that he was about to tell the new owners what she wanted. They all went out into the old walled garden then, and it was on one of its narrow paths while passing by a clump of old boles of quince, among which the gardener was working (as much as he ever did), that the Marquis dropped behind and said to his daughter: 'All that it is necessary for him to know about the house I shall tell him.'

"And she said, 'But, Father, you must tell him about the curse.'

" 'No,' he said in such a way that she might have seen that further words were useless, 'we have borne it for ten generations, so they can now.'

" 'We!' she said. 'But we are of steel, steel of Toledo. How will they ever . . .' but he would have no more of it: he was hit too hard by the loss of Casa Viljeros to be capable of ordinary right sympathies; and his daughter saw that she could do nothing more for the strangers that were so light-heartedly entering her home. And the other daughter dared say nothing at all. If any more was said there is no trace of it.

"That evening with the last of the light the Viljeros family lumbered away in a wonderful old carriage, and the Americans entered the house with a few servants, and the hounds arrived and were well enough housed in the stables.

"They had dinner cheerily enough, but for the gradual approach of a certain uneasiness; and then they went to sit in the long library, which was lighted now by nearly a gross of candles. For a little while they walked round the room, looking at the faces of the satyrs carved on great chests and cupboards, and wondering what romances slept through the ages wrapped in their blackened leather along the shelves. But soon they found that they were going on tip-toe, and knew from this they were offending against the hush, and sat down and spoke in whispers. They seemed to think that, if they sat still for a while, the silence brooding among the shadows would pass. Yet it was far otherwise, for the frowns on the faces of the satyrs seemed rather to increase in grimness, and every shadow that slipped from its place as a candle flickered began to look like a warning. And when Easel went out and got twenty or thirty more candles, the shadows that were driven further away seemed only to gather together with grimmer intent in the corners. Soon it seemed they were boding something, seemed that whenever you caught one of the dark corners with the tail of your eye it was threatening you, a warning you only lost when you looked straight at it. Look straight at it then, the reader may say. But which was right, the straight gaze or the tail of the eye? And while you looked straight at one sinister shadow, there were dozens more all round that went on with their warnings. They spoke little of all this, scarce spoke at all, all waiting for the strangeness of the house, as they called it, to go away; but nothing material or immaterial left that house after the old hidalgo and his daughters had rocked away down the road in their wonderful carriage. Here they were in the long library with whatever the ages had given to that dark house: travellers across the Atlantic might come and go, but the mystery of Casa Viljeros kept house with its own communion of shadows. As the candles burned lower imperceptible changes occurred in the shadow assembly;

some grew taller, some blacker, but one and all seemed to grow, and the whole room with them, more menacing, more foreboding, more sure of a doom. They got fresh candles and the three men carried them all over the room, sending the darker shadows scurrying away from their lurking-places; they had done it to cheer the women, and to show they were not afraid, but the leaping shadows driven from their old corners brought anything but cheer, and all the Stolger family knew that things were going badly with their new possession if it had come already to showing they were not afraid. And very soon they came back to their chairs and all moved closer together; and the shadows slipped back to their places and the menace was deeper yet.

"Had they spoken they knew that things would have been better, that the echoes of their own voices might have been stronger than whatever it was that they would not yet put a name to; and this they tried to do, but by now they were all of them speaking only in whispers. They should have spoken out, they should have shouted, they should have told stale jokes or sung common songs, and they might have set up some sort of a rampart from scraps of the twentieth century to hold back this ancient thing, whatever it was, that was filling the room with terror; but they spoke in whispers, and that dark influence came at them right down the ages. And hour by hour it grew in intensity. I suppose they were afraid to go to bed. Midnight found them still there, sitting all close together, and the menace of the unknown influence deeper. Easel, the youngest, had at one time drawn his revolver, but the moment he did it he saw himself what a childish act it was; the revolver looked so sharp of outline and shiny among the vague forms of those threatening shadows. And the leers seemed to deepen upon the lips of the satyrs. With the flare of a candle, with the sudden turn of an eye, a few letters of faded gilt would light up now and then on the back of some sombre book, half a word of Spanish whispering without meaning out of the years that were troubling them, and blinking away with its warning all untold.

"A few more candles had been collected now and then, until they saw that by multiplying candles they only multiplied shadows, and that there was something more in the gloom than what could be driven away by a few of these little flames. They saw too, or felt or knew, that whatever darkness the candles drove back from the little circle in which they sat huddled together only lurked just out of sight behind some edge of old timber, waiting to stalk out upon them as soon as the candles dwindled, surely and swiftly in all the majesty of their darkness.

"It was not the dwindling of the candles, it was not any fading of the light from their flames, that brought a great change after midnight; it was something that lay in the very shadows themselves, something that earlier in the night had been dormant, or not ascertainable by human emotions, and that was now active and stirring and not to be overlooked by human fears. Against this terror they did nothing further now, carried no more candles about, drew out no more youthful revolvers, but recognized themselves in the grip of some influence against which such things were idle. And the curse, for such it was, gloomed, multiplied and foreboded; and there they sat, a little castaway group, lost as though the twentieth century had suddenly foundered, amidst an encroaching power from an age of which they knew nothing.

"What were they to do? As the night went on the curse grew stronger and darker, as though the witch that had anciently laid it upon that house were forcing it down on it with both hands, mass upon mass of it out of dark and dangerous air; while out of the shadows rose up those oaken satyrs larger than man, with scorn on their carven lips. What could they do if they daren't leave that little circle in which they sat close together in the brightest part of the room, and daren't speak louder than whisperings? More and more ominous grew the shadows. And then Hendrik speaking out loud said to his father: 'Look here, Dad, I've travelled in South America; I know magic when I see it. And I've seen something of witchcraft. There's a curse here, in this room; there's no doubt of it.'

"They all started a bit at that. And Hendrik went on. 'Well, I'm only putting it into words,' he said. 'Don't you all feel it?'

"They had nothing to say to that: they could not say it was not so.

" 'Let's take the car over to Hurgos,' he said. 'They've an hotel there called the Annunciation. Let's live there. And let's start now.'

"And at that moment the hounds, that were never quite easy in their new kennels, gave tongue at the moon. And Hendrik went on: 'Let's keep the hounds in here, to show them what we think of their Spanish curses.'

" 'In the library?' said his father.

"And all Hendrik answered was: 'They ought to have told us there was something wrong about the damned place.'

" 'But why should it affect us?' said his father.

" 'Well, doesn't it?' said Hendrik.

"And that they found unanswerable.

"With one speaking his mind and the rest only whispering, you can easily guess how it went. 'We can come over whenever we want,' Hendrik explained. 'It mayn't be so bad by day.'

"They went there and then. And they turned the hounds into the library as Hendrik had said.

"Why the witch laid that curse all those ages ago I never enquired of the gardener, nor what exactly it was. But I felt I knew something of it myself, though it could not be put into words, from listening to those hounds all night in the library. Something was there that they knew of and told to the night, and too much book-learning and living in towns had blunted my ears to the sense of it. It was something that . . . but no words of mine can make it clear to you now. You should have heard those hounds a mile away over the moor, howling, howling, howling."

Hunting the Unicorn

To say that amongst all those that have read any of the tales of Mr. Jorkens' travels that I have recorded, none has felt any doubts of any of them would be absurd: such doubts have been felt and even expressed. But what has impressed me very considerably is the fair-minded attitude taken up by the general public, an attitude that may be summarized as a firm determination not to disbelieve a man's story merely because it is unusual, but to await the final verdict of science when science shall have arrived at the point at which it is able to pronounce on such matters with certainty. Then, should the verdict be against Jorkens, and not till then, will a sporting public turn upon him that scornful disbelief that they are far too fair-minded to show without good and sufficient proofs. I myself meanwhile am careful to record nothing he tells me, against which anyone in the Billiards Club or elsewhere has been able to bring any proof that would definitely rule it out in a court of law. And it would be interesting to see for how long in such a court arguments that may be lightly advanced now, against the exact truth of any one of his tales, would stand up against the ridicule of counsel. But the sporting attitude that the public have adopted towards him is more to Jorkens than a verdict in any court of law. Curiously enough it is in the Billiards Club itself, the source of all these stories, that the most unsporting attitude is often shown to Jorkens. For instance only the other day one of our members was unnecessarily rude to him, though with only a single word. I need hardly say it was Terbut. The word was not in itself a rude one, but was somehow all the more insidious for

214

that. Also it was really a single word, and not a short sentence, as is often the case when a writer says to you "I will tell it to you in one word." But I will tell the story.

We were discussing billiards, which is not a thing we often do in the Billiards Club. There is, I suppose, some sort of feeling that, if anyone talks of billiards there, his imagination or his experience can provide him with nothing better; billiards being, as it were, bed-rock in the Billiards Club. In just the same way at the Athenaeum, although the bird is inseparable from the Club's presiding goddess, one seldom, if ever, orders an owl for one's lunch. But we were discussing billiards today, and debating whether bonzoline balls or the old ivory kind were the better. I will not record the discussion, for it has nothing to do with Jorkens, but it may interest my readers to hear that it was held at the Billiards Club that the bonzoline ball was unique among modern substitutes, in being better than the old genuine article. It was as we had decided that, that some young member who ought to have known better, seeing Jorkens near him as he looked up, suddenly blurted out: "Have you ever seen a unicorn, Jorkens?"

Of course it was not the way to speak to an elder man. Of course the implication was obvious. And Jorkens saw in a moment that the young fellow did not believe in the existence of unicorns at all. In any case he had not yet passed that time of life, in which one believes nothing that the ages have handed down to us until we have been able to test it for ourselves.

"I deprecate that hard and fast line between fabulous animals and those that you all chance to have seen," said Jorkens. "What does it amount to, practically, but a line drawn round Regent's Park? That's all it is really. Everything inside that line is an animal you readily believe in. Everything outside it is fabulous. It means you believe in an animal if you have seen it in the Zoo, otherwise not. However full history is of accounts of the unicorn, and the most detailed descriptions, still you go off to Regent's Park on a Sunday, and if there is not one there waiting for your bun you disbelieve in the unicorn. Oh well, I was like that myself till I saw one."

"You saw one?" said the young fellow who had started the topic.

"I'll tell you," said Jorkens.

"I was camped once by the Northern Guaso Nyero, or rather I was camped two hundred and fifty yards from it, a distance that just makes all the difference, for two hundred yards is all that the mosquito flies from his home. Of course he has a good many homes, that's the trouble; but, as he prefers a river frontage, it's a very good thing to camp that far from a river. Not that it amounts to much, for Africa can always get you some other way. But there it was. Well, I was collecting heads for a museum, and had been at it for some time, with a white hunter and eighty natives, trekking through Africa; and I was beginning to get pretty tired of it. I was sitting by one of our campfires after supper, with the white hunter beside me, and I was gazing into the glow of the smouldering logs and watching the fireflies gliding backwards and forwards, and thinking all the while of the lights of London. And the more the fireflies slowly grew into multitudes, and the more the fire glowed, the more I longed for London. In that mood I asked the hunter what we should do next day; and, whatever he suggested going after, I pointed out I had shot it already. Which was perfectly true.

"And winds came out of the forest, or over the plains, and softly played with the smoke going up from our logs of cedar, and the visions changed and changed in the glow of the fire, and every now and then the hunter would make some new suggestion, till I said petulantly: 'Find me something I haven't shot yet.'

"And he said: 'Very well, I will.'

"'What is it?' I said.

"And he wouldn't say.

"I kept on asking him, but he wouldn't tell me. The man whose job it was, the askari we called him, came and put more logs on the fire, and we sat on long with little cold winds on our backs and the warmth on our hands and feet, but still he would not say. 'Why not?' I asked him at last. 'Because you'd think me mad,' he said. 'Well, aren't you?' I asked. Partly my insinuation was true, and partly it was the product of some unreasonable irritation that had come over me, and Africa was responsible for both.

"Next day he moved our camp to the edge of the river, and we waited there a long time; I don't remember how long, quite a fortnight; and all the while he stuck to his promise to find me this new beast that I had never shot.

"I began to get malaria, and so did he. And then one night as we were talking of remedies, for we were both tired of quinine, he told me what it was we were looking for. Yes, simply a unicorn. He had had natives out in the forest searching for it for weeks, and though they had not yet seen it they had at last found the spoor. And then he explained to me about how to get a unicorn. The animal, he explained to me, was always fairly cautious of men, and on the whole, in spite of exceptions, had tended to avoid them more than do other animals; but that of late centuries, probably since the invention of fire-arms, or since some other change in the ways of men, it had avoided men so assiduously that it had almost dropped out of history. Up to the time that a Pope gave the horn of one to King François one day in the fifteenth century, and for a while after, references to the unicorn are so frequent that its avoidance of man, however much wished by the unicorn, can only be called unsuccessful; after that time a cunning unknown before seems to have been added to its love of elusiveness, with the result that it is no longer classed among European mammals. And then the hunter explained to me how to get one. There was no way whatever to come at him, he explained, except one, and that was to drive him. And then he drew out some paper and a bit of pencil, and showed me how it was done: he made a row of dots in a semi-circle to represent beaters, and put a cross in the middle to mark the unicorn, and showed me how the flanks came gradually in. His hand was rather shaky with malaria, and I couldn't see very well either, but the thing seemed simple enough, a perfectly ordinary beat.

" 'Yes, I see,' I said, 'and the gun stands here.' And I pointed to a place ahead of the unicorn, to which the semi-circle of beaters was moving.

" 'No,' he said. 'That would do for any other animal; but not for the unicorn. It's been tried, and that's why nobody ever gets one. With the unicorn avoidance of man amounts to a passion. Whatever it was in the past, that's what it is now; and not to take account of that is an error as great as supposing a rhino can't smell. The moment the unicorn sees the line of beaters, with the flanks coming quietly in on him he knows what's up; he knows he's being driven. By a glance at the line (and his sight is very acute) he knows to what direction. He immediately slips through the forest in exactly the opposite; straight through the line of beaters; and in these forests he usually gets through without even being seen by a native. Not that they haven't seen them.'

" 'Then the place for a gun to stand,' I said.

" 'Exactly,' he interrupted. 'Stand in front of the unicorn, wherever he is, and we'll try to drive him away from you. He's sure to come straight back.'

"Now this seemed to me perfectly sound. Unicorns do avoid men, there can be no doubt of that. They must have some method in doing it. Granting a considerable intelligence, without which no method is any good, what better than hiding in a dense forest, and, when driven, always going in the opposite direction to that which is obviously intended. And history is too full of the unicorn for us to suppose that they are merely not there.

" 'Well,' said Rhino, for Rhino Parks was his name there, whatever it may have been in England once, 'those Wakamba trackers have found him. What about trying tomorrow?'

" 'I'm not sure that I can hold a rifle just yet,' I said.

" 'No use giving in to malaria here,' he answered, 'or no one would ever do anything.'

"Which is true, though the place is a good deal written up as a health-resort.

" 'All right. Tomorrow,' I said.

"And tomorrow came, which was one thing to the good. You never know what's coming, with malaria.

"Well I was up and ready by five, but Rhino wouldn't start till I'd had a good breakfast. So I sat down to it. It had to be liquid, because I could have no more eaten bacon and eggs, as I was just then, than I could have eaten a live squirrel. But we made a breakfast of sorts on two bottles of vermuth that we had; and by about seven we started.

"And now comes the incredible part of my story: we crossed the river and pushed into the forest, and I took up my place where the Wakambas told me in whispers, and the beaters moved off away from me, and all the while I had forgotten to load my rifle. You may not believe me; and, if you don't, I don't wonder; but there it was, I did it. Malaria I suppose. As a matter of fact it is just one of those things that people do do once in their lives, and very often of course it happens to be the last thing they ever do. Well, I stood there with my rifle empty, waiting for the unicorn, a .360 magazine: the magazine holds five cartridges, and there should be another one in the barrel: and the steps of the beaters sounded further and further away from me. And then there came a broken furtive sound, as of something heavy but sly coming down through the forest. And there I was, with my empty rifle ready. And all of a sudden I saw a great shoulder so graceful, so silken and gleaming white, close by in that denseness of greenery, that I knew that it must be the unicorn. Of course I'd seen hundreds of pictures of them, and the thing that I marvelled at most was that the beast, or all I could see of him, was so surprisingly like to the pictures.

I put up my rifle and took a good enough aim, and then click, and I knew it was empty.

"Of course I hadn't forgotten to bring any cartridges at all, I wasn't so crazy as that, whatever my temperature was: my pocket was full of them. I put my hand to my pocket and slipped in a cartridge at once, and there I was loaded, with the unicorn still only twenty-five yards away. But he had heard the click, and, whether or not he knew what it was, he at any rate knew it for man, even if he hadn't yet seen me; and he changed at once his slow slinking glide for a sharp trot through the forest. Again in a gap I saw a flash of his whiteness, and I fired and am sure I hit him, and then he came for me. Where I hit him I never knew, my one good chance of a shot behind the shoulder was gone, and I had had to take whatever shot I could get; and now I was again unloaded, for there had been no time to put anything into the magazine, and the unicorn was practically on top of me. Even as I took another cartridge out of my pocket he made a lunge at me with his flashing horn, a deadly weapon of ivory. I parried it with my rifle, and only barely parried, for the strength of its neck was enormous. It wasn't a thing that you could waft aside as you can with the thrust of a sword, if only you are in time; it was so gigantic a thrust that it took all one's strength to turn it. And you had to be just as quick as when trying to parry a rapier; even quicker. At once he lunged again, and again I parried: no question of thinking of trying to load my rifle; there was only just time for the parry. And as I barely parried, and the horn slipped by under my left arm, through the brown shirt I was wearing, clean as a bullet, I knew that I should parry few more, if any, like that; and that with the next thrust, or the one after, all would be over; for the power I felt in that horn was clearly more than my match. So I stepped back to gain an instant; which I barely did, so swiftly the huge beast stepped forward; and then I swung my rifle over my back and before he thrust again I brought it down as hard as I could at his head. I knew it for my last chance, and put into it all the strength that malaria had left me. Now it was his turn to parry. He saw it coming and flicked at it with his horn, and the horn caught it and the two blows came together. Either of them was a good blow. And together they amounted to pretty much of a smash. Well, neither ivory nor steel is unbreakable; and as for the stock of my rifle I don't know where it went: the branches all round were full of flying splinters. And then I saw that long thin murderous horn lying white on the ground beside me. The unicorn saw it too: it put its forefeet out, and lowered its nose and sniffed at it. As the beast was doing nothing at the moment, I picked the horn up. And when it saw the horn in my hand it looked irresolutely at me. For a moment we stood like that. It might easily have overcome me by sheer weight, and trampled me under with its pointed hooves; and yet it stood there motionless, seeming to have an awe for its own horn, which it now saw turned against it. Then I moved the horn into the hand that was holding the rifle, with the intention of seeing if it was possible to get a cartridge into what was left of the breech; and at the movement of the horn in my hand the unicorn shied like a horse, then turned round and kicked out with his heels and sprang away, and was almost immediately lost to sight in the forest. And that was the last I ever saw of a unicorn."

"But the horn," said the young fellow who had asked at first about unicorns. "Why didn't you keep the horn?"

"Waiter," said Jorkens without a word to his critic, "bring me that toasting fork that I gave to the Club."

We most of us present something to the Club, and sure enough Jorkens had once given an ivory-handled toasting fork, that lay in a drawer in the pantry; for whoever wants to use a toasting fork in a Club? And now the waiter brought it, a fork with silver prongs, or electro-plate, and a long ivory handle, too narrow for the tusk of an elephant and too long for a tooth. "And bring me," he said, "a small whiskey and soda."

The whiskey was brought, and as he drank it the strange fork was handed round. Not all of us had seen it before; none of us had eyed it attentively.

"Well, what do you make of it?" said Jorkens when he had finished his whiskey.

It was then that Terbut leaned over to me and whispered, but only too audibly, the one word "Bonzoline."

The ungenerous comment cast over the table something like, well, a miasma. And that's the kind of thing that Jorkens has to put up with.

The Pale-Green Image

So heavy was the gloom one afternoon in the Billiards Club, that I wondered why the waiters did not turn on the lights. The darkness clung in cornices and seemed to beat down from the ceiling, and it was only low near the floor that we had any light at all. Some were for putting on the lights at once, but others felt that that would be to surrender the day, before it was yet three, to the forces of fog and night. Luckily it is this very thing that so often encourages Jorkens to turn his memories eastwards into the sunlight; and though merely turning them that way does not inspire him to talk, a whiskey-and-soda always will, and it was at this juncture that I offered him one.

"When I was in Tunis," Jorkens said, "I had an experience that may be of interest to some of you. Well, it was in London that the thing all came to a head; so I had better begin there. It was at the Ecclesiastical Club, and I was a member in those days. The members are not all bishops by any means; there are plenty of laity there, plenty of men who never sung a hymn in their lives; but, at the same time, pretty nearly every bishop belongs to it. Well, there was a fellow called Purry, a nasty sort of fellow, and he did a nasty sort of thing; a thing that nobody had ever done in the Ecclesiastical Club before, or in any other club, I should think. He brought up a bishop before the committee, for them to enquire into his conduct. Yes, that is what he did. Naturally the committee of the Ecclesiastical Club saw what a disgraceful thing it was that Purry was doing, and tried to explain it to him; but Purry wouldn't see it. He was one of those devilish ferreting fellows that know

223

more about the rules of a club than the committee do. And in the end he got them to do it; got them to haul up the bishop before them, I mean."

"But how on earth could he do that?" said most of us.

"Well," said Jorkens when our exclamations subsided, "he had ferreted out that the bishop, who had gone for a holiday to Tunis, had been driving a small car and there had been a fatal accident. An Arab, you know. Well, the committee made one last effort to make Purry see what a blackguard he was, and then they hauled up the bishop just as he told them. The defence was hardly left in the hands of the bishop: the president of the committee practically did that for himself. He said everybody knew the bishop, and everybody knew what Arabs were. And both those statements went down with the committee so tremendously, that they almost decided the case without any more talk. A further point that was made in the bishop's favour was that the judiciary of the country concerned had acquitted him; and another point was that he had paid a hundred pounds compensation to the Arab's family, which in Tunis goes a very long way. Then the committee apologized to the bishop, very much as though they had murdered his mother; and nothing then remained to be done but to get rid of Purry, which was no easy thing to do, and it took us a year to do it. But we couldn't have a man like that in the Club. Finally we caught him under a byelaw; and a difficult job it was, as I said. How on earth he got hold of the story I never knew, and I don't know to this day, and I never shall; but he was one of those ferreting fellows that grub things up."

"Read it in the papers, I should imagine," said Terbut, "if it came before the courts. No great difficulty in getting hold of a paper from Tunis."

"Oh, he needn't have got it from Tunis," said Jorkens. "It was copied at the time into all the English papers. But he must have known more than that. That damned fellow Purry must have found out what really happened. And I thought I was the only living man who knew, not counting the bishop. How Purry got hold of it is an eternal mystery."

"And what did really happen?" asked Terbut.

"What really happened," said Jorkens, "was that I was taking a walk one day in the souks, a queer covered lane with shops on both sides of it all the way along. So far as I can remember, the shops have no windows or doors: they all look out on the lane, and you pass through hundreds of yards of merchandise. In one of these shops was an Arab called Amool ben Ibrahim, who had all kinds of things to sell; carpets mostly; and a queer little image of duck's-egg green, which he was too eager to sell me. I don't know what it was made of; enamelled copper perhaps, six inches high and less than an inch thick. When I saw that he was too eager to sell it to me, I rather sheered off from it.

"We got to know each other quite well and drank a great deal of coffee together, as one does in that land if one has any business to do; and if one has no business, and time hangs heavy, one drinks coffee just the same; black coffee with the ground berry filling a third of the little cup. I never taste it here. If I could get one cup of that coffee, it would bring back the East to me like a vision; Tunis, the Roman ruins and the date-palms, and beyond them the boundless desert."

"You were saying, Jorkens . . . ?" I interposed.

"Ah yes, the souks," said Jorkens. "Well one day I said I would buy that pale-green image after all, and then the Arab wouldn't sell it. Well, I increased my price, as one does; but still he wouldn't sell. Of course I saw there was some queer story there, and we had some more coffee and he told it to me. And this was the story: a curse went with the image. Well, that wasn't so new to me as it might be to you. I knew the East a bit. I just asked Amool what kind of curse it was. And Amool told me. It worked like this: when you came by that pale-green image of some old god of the Nile; an image of the days of ignorance Amool called it, by which he meant the ages before Mahomet; when you bought this thing, it dominated your life, gripped your ideas, and never let go of them. That meant you had no rest, no leisure, no peace of mind; and the only thing to do was to sell it, as he had once tried to sell it to me, and as now he would not; or else shake off its power in the other way; which he was not able to do. That was the curse, and the methods of shaking it off were very easy. They were lightly cut into the sides of the image in all manner of languages. It was simply this: that the man who bought the image had to kill the man that he bought it from; at least, he was very strongly impelled to do so; and, when he did so, all his troubles ceased. That was the situation, and he had bought the accursed thing from a Touareg, who had ridden in from the desert to sell it, and might now be with his camel a thousand miles away, besides being a bad fellow to follow in any case. So he had to sell it, and what was he to do? I asked him for another lump of sugar, and I drank my coffee down to the lovely dregs; and then the idea came to me. 'Our people,' I said to Amool, 'are not like the Touaregs, and some are not even like the Arabs. We have men among us who kill nobody.'

" 'Nobody?' said Amool.

" 'Under no circumstances,' I said.

" 'And if one of them had but two wives,' said Amool, 'and a man came and took both away from him on the one day, such a man as you tell of would not smite even then?'

" 'Not even then,' I said, passing over the detail of the two wives, for a lesson upon monogamy would only have puzzled Amool.

" 'And such a one of your people is here in Tunis?' asked he.

" 'The very man,' I said.

"It was the Bishop of Britchester: he was in the same hotel as I was, and I had met him.

" 'I will bring such a man to you,' I said to Amool, 'and you shall sell him the image, and under no circumstances will he kill you.'

"Of that I felt certain, and I felt almost equally sure that no heathen spells could affect an English bishop. Well, of course I was wrong. I didn't know the strength of the spell, or perhaps the strength of the bishop. I don't suppose I was wrong about the bishop: I imagine he had the strength to resist any temptation that could come to a man in England. It was the spell I was wrong about.

"There is not much more to tell. I brought the bishop around to Amool's shop: everybody goes to the souks to see the carpets, so there was no difficulty in getting him there. I had got Amool to agree to any price whatever that I thought best; and having headed the bishop towards the image, I cast the price at him like a fly.

"Well, I made one man happy.

"But he wasn't happy for long: the accident, as of course one must always call it, in which the Bishop's car was concerned, occurred in under a week; and that was the end of poor Amool ben Ibrahim. But how that blackguard Purry got to hear of it is one of those secrets that perhaps make life more interesting, but which we shall never know."

The Sacred City of Krakovlitz

There was always something a bit wild about the odd hill of which this story tells; there were myrtle bushes dotted about it, which gave it a wild air, and shrubs of other kinds and a few large lonely rocks, and all the little things by which hills so often proclaim that, unlike the fields and gardens, they owe no allegiance to Man. It was a bit wild in any case, without the mirage; so that when the mirage came, shining down on the top of it, and putting over the myrtles, azaleas and junipers a little eastern city, such as could not have possibly stood within a hundred miles, then it was no wonder that a young impressionable peasant of that far end of Europe that we call the Near East considered the hill sacred.

He was watching a herd of nine or ten goats amongst the herbage that straggled about the base of the hill, when the mirage shone there, a mass of white domes gleaming above white walls, with thin towers among them, and tiny gold spires on the tops of some of the domes; very compact and small, a little city exactly fitting the top of the hill. It did not shine there for more than twenty minutes, but while it was there it was very clear indeed. It is rather a desolate district, that of Krakovlitz, and no living creature was in sight of Srebzt besides his herd of goats. It is doubtful if any saw the mirage but he, though several said they did afterwards. All the time it was there, Srebzt stood and gazed at it with enormous wonder. He had never seen an oriental city. I do not know by what means light picks up such visions from where they are real and puts them down again somewhere where they are not. It very rarely happens. Everything that ever occurs among the simple people dwelling round Krakovlitz drifts into legend, to be handed down through the ages; and there is no record of anything of the sort having occurred there before for nearly two hundred years. The previous event is exactly dated, because legend tells how it occurred on the eve of a battle, and the battle has its place and its date in history.

As Srebzt gazed at the very vivid mirage, the whole city was deeply impressed upon his mind; and it was so new to him, and so strangely beautiful, that for twenty minutes his eye roved over its details, going from house to house, and from walled garden to walled garden, where palm trees put their heads here and there above the tops of the walls. It was quite obviously a city of people following no religion of Srebzt's; but, after all, his faith had come from the East, and the city was obviously eastern. And all at once it appeared to him holy. He ran up the hill towards it as far as he could, but that was not far, for very soon he came to the royal wall, which enclosed the greater part of the hill within the Demesne of the Palace, a wild park in which goats were forbidden.

The first impression of the city, seen in a flash, the beauty and wonder of it, and then the examination of every building, and the feeling that it was holy coming on top of that, combined to give Srebzt a vision of that city, clear and exact in its details, which never faded. Perhaps no missionary has ever treasured a clearer picture of Heaven than was the picture of the mirage on the top of the hill of Krakovlitz, stamped upon Srebzt's memory. In fact the picture made Srebzt into a missionary: he went through all the villages, and even as far as towns, telling them of the city upon the hill and swearing that it was sacred and that it was more beautiful than any city of earth, as it certainly was prettier than any town that he can ever have had opportunities of beholding. And, though it had faded after twenty minutes, he always spoke of it to the people of all the villages as though it were still there and would never leave the hill. He became a familiar figure in all the country round, in market-places at evening, or in whatever little spaces in the middle of villages were empty when work was over, where men could gather and talk.

A hundred miles from Krakovlitz in many directions they knew his flapping cloak, his outstretched arm and his vehement declamations; for he walked great distances, and would cover a hundred miles in three or four days. And everywhere he said the same thing, that the earth was corrupt and its governments were corrupt, but that on the top of the hill of Krakovlitz shone the serene beauty of the utterly perfect city, and that the laws that ran in its streets were the laws of Heaven. Some believed him, some went to Krakovlitz to see for themselves, and of course saw nothing; but such fiery oratory soon came to have more weight with them than their eyesight, till they too believed. The simple people of the country round Krakovlitz are easily excited, and the torrent of words in the twilight, poured out at them, often, till all the stars were lit, and the unquestioned sincerity of Srebzt, carried them all away, and they believed that on the top of Krakovlitz hill all the highest ideals of men blossomed incorruptibly in a city of unimaginable beauty, seen by one man. But all but the fields at the very base of the hill were in the Demesne of the Palace, and the domes and the golden spires could not be seen from the fields below, being, as Srebzt taught, too lofty for human eye, and the Government would not permit the people to go up the slopes of Krakovlitz.

And so things were for a long time; a fierce religious revival, or heresy if you will, among tens of thousands of peasantry, and, on the side of the government, law, routine and materialism. This could not last for ever. There were arrests, imprisonments and one execution, and after the execution the whole revival flared up and lengths of the royal wall were battered down and Srebzt led all the people up the slope of the hill; but not all the way: he halted them soon and went up to the top alone, and came back and told them that he had seen the city, but that it was not yet material, not yet gross enough for their eyes. It was a strangely mystical speech, the speech in which he told them that the city that he had just seen, and in which he had just walked, was truly there for good men, and yet not so completely there for others.

I cannot explain this exact theory; nor, I think, could he have done so in broad daylight, but the long shadows of evening had died from the rock and the bushes, and twilight, in spite of the multitude, had become strangely hushed and the sky was full of some very glorious colours; and Srebzt called to them in the stillness, almost chanting, telling them of the wonders of the city that he had seen, and which they too should see, if they were just and pure and patriotic and, above all, obedient. And they did see it. For the government fled that night, and Srebzt assumed power next morning. And the first thing he did was to collect all the builders in the country and, cleverly enough, to get architects from abroad, even though he taught that foreigners were all perfectly useless; and, with his intense vision burning as clearly as ever in his fanatical memory, he really did succeed in a very few months in having the city of the mirage duplicated exactly. And he moved into the city with his ministers and made it the seat of government, as everyone knows.

Not everyone knew what the workmen had done; not everyone even knew that there had been workmen at all, for they were a very simple people, and the sight of the city gleaming upon the hill, and exactly as Srebzt had described it, clinched once for all in their minds the divine vision of Srebzt. If there was a single doubter upon this point in the whole of the country, he was invariably silent.

The power of Srebzt was now absolute, and from this point onward is merely a matter of history. To go further with this story would be to attempt to stir with one's pen the turbulent waters of European diplomacy, and would be to repeat unnecessarily events well known to the world, a world so troubled that it already forgets those early stages of Srebzt's assumption of power.

And yet I know that the story is true, for my friend Jorkens told it to me one day at the Billiards Club, and he has travelled everywhere and knows many a thing which the hurried world forgets. And I have not only Jorkens' bare word for it; for no sooner had he ceased telling the tale after lunch, when from the other side of the table came immediate corroboration. Sillet, one of our members, had been a subadministrator in the East; the real East, not the Near East, many hundreds of miles beyond Krakovlitz. And there had been a town in his subadministration, called Loom-bah; and Sillet, who was a man of very few words, told his story in very few words. He had been dissatisfied with Loom-bah. Odd though it may seem to us, there were the most appalling vices, and even some kinds of murder, which Sillet put up with; but there were certain kinds of murder he never would tolerate, and several of these were taking place in Loom-bah. He decided to stop it; decided, in his own words, "to tidy up the town"; and found that he could not do it. Sillet persisted and, again to use his own words, "I decided rightly or wrongly that the best thing would be to burn it." So he called out the military, for which there was ample provocation at any time, and did burn Loom-bah.

And then for many years the thing had been on his conscience, although he could see no other way of stopping these foul murders that used to go on in Loom-bah, and of which, as he said, there were a great deal too many. As an official he approved of what he had done, but then there was some unofficial part of him that, in spite of the crimes of Loom-bah, was unreasonably yearning to see that quaint small city again. And the knowledge that he had acted rightly could not keep him from feeling sorry. He had done it quite thoroughly, and nothing at all was left of Loom-bah. And then one day he came home from the East by motor, and of course he passed through the Near East; and, as it happened, he went right by Krakovlitz, where the ruins of the royal wall were being used for mending the road, which the old regime used never to mend at all. And on the top of the hill he saw Loom-bah, with Srebzt's flag flying from the dome of a mosque.

"It was perfectly exact," he said, "a view of Loom-bah from the south. I knew every house in it. I had arrested somebody in every street, and I had been myself into every house to get evidence about some murder or other, and I couldn't have been mistaken."

Then we talked awhile about mirages, all giving our own theories. We pulled out an atlas and found where Loom-bah was, though the actual name was not marked, and we drew a line from it to Krakovlitz, which was marked under its old name, and we measured the line and worked out the angle that it made with another line that we drew from Loom-bah to the magnetic pole, thinking that that might have something to do with it. And Sillet had seen mirages himself, on several occasions, though he did not know how they worked. And he had no more to say, and Jorkens was now asleep, and we could think of no more theories.

"But it was Loom-bah, all right," said Sillet, "however it got there."

At Sunset

I would go in, for it is growing cold.
   Yet, if I go, that colour on the sea
   May turn to something never known to me;
Those godlike shapes among the sunset's gold
May grow more magical; some light untold
   May gleam upon the houses suddenly;
   Some mystery I had not thought could be
This evening in a moment may unfold.

For fleeting moments wonderfully bright
   Make up life's treasury; such gems as these
   Are all the spirit on its way can seize,
Moving across the world from night to night;
   And are the only jewels it can show
   To other ghosts, wherever it may go.

       LORD DUNSANY
       July 24, 1878–October 25, 1957.

The World's Best Adult Fantasy

Ballantine Books

$1.25 each

To order by mail, send $1.25 per book plus 25¢ per order for handling to Ballantine Cash Sales, P.O. Box 505, Westminster, Maryland 21157. Please allow three weeks for delivery.

CLASSIC
ADULT FANTASY

FROM
BALLANTINE BOOKS

* The Gormenghast Trilogy

To order by mail, send $1.25 per book plus 25¢
per order for handling to Ballantine Cash Sales,
P.O. Box 505, Westminster, Maryland 21157.
Please allow three weeks for delivery.

"In the range of imaginative literature, Lovecraft created a new form. His work is both lore and legend at their haunting best."—August Derleth

H. P. LOVECRAFT

THE TOMB and Other Tales
Stories and sketches in HPL's most characteristic style, including the keystone Cthulhu story, "The Festival," and his last story, "The Wicked Clergyman."

AT THE MOUNTAINS OF MADNESS and Other Tales of Terror
Lovecraft's finest short novel of the horror that dwelt in the frozen Antarctic, plus such classic chillers as "Dreams in the Witch-House" and "The Shunned House."

THE LURKING FEAR and Other Stories
Twelve of his most remarkable tales, including the famous "Shadow Over Innsmouth."

THE SHUTTERED ROOM and Other Tales of Horror (with August Derleth)
Stories of dread secrets and mind-wrenching terror beyond the borders of experience.

TALES OF THE CTHULHU MYTHOS, Volume 1
The classic "Call of Cthulhu" plus stories by other writers inspired by the Mythos—Long, Howard, Derleth, et al.

TALES OF THE CTHULHU MYTHOS, Volume 2
In addition to Lovecraft's classic "The Haunter of the Dark," this volume includes stories by Bloch, Wilson and others.

To order by mail, send 95¢ per book plus 25¢ per order for handling to Ballantine ash Sales, P.O. Box 505, Westminster, Maryland 21157. Please allow three weeks for delivery.

Edgar Rice Burroughs

MARS NOVELS

To order by mail send $1.25 per book plus
25¢ per order for handling to Ballantine Cash
Sales, P.O. Box 505, Westminster, Maryland
21157. Please allow three weeks for delivery.

The great masterpieces of fantasy by
J. R. R. TOLKIEN

The Hobbit
and
The Lord of the Rings

Part I—The Fellowship of the Ring

Part II—The Two Towers

Part III—The Return of the King

Note: These are the complete and authorized paper-bound editions, published only by Ballantine Books.